Writing About Art

Writing About Art

Sixth Edition

Henry M. Sayre
Oregon State University

PEARSON
Prentice
Hall

Upper Saddle River, New Jersey 07458

Library of Congress Cataloging-in-Publication Data

Sayre, Henry M.,
  Writing about art / Henry M. Sayre. —6th ed.
    p. cm.
  Includes bibliographical references and index.
  ISBN 978-0-205-64578-7
1. Art criticism—Authorship. I. Title.
  N7476.S29 2009
  808'.0667—dc22

                                    2008016670

Editor in Chief: Sarah Touborg
Editorial Assistant: Carla Worner
Senior Editor: Amber Mackey
Editorial Project Manager: Alexandra Huggins
Director of Marketing: Tim Stookesberry
Executive Marketing Manager: Wendy Gordon
Senior Managing Editor: Mary Rottino
Production Liaison: Jean Lapidus
Composition/Full-Service Management:
  Prepare/Emilcomp
Production Editor: Francesca Monaco
Senior Operations Supervisor: Brian Mackey
Color Scanning: Cory Skidds
Manager, Visual Research: Beth Brenzel
Image Permission Coordinator:
  Debbie Latronica
Manager, Visual Research & Permissions:
  Karen Sanatar
Image Permission Coordinator: Rita Wenning

Cover Design: Bruce Kenselaar
Front Cover Art: Sean Scully, *Vincent*, 2002.
  Oil, acrylic, and gouache on canvas,
  75 in. × 80 in. Source: Sean Scully,
  Wall of Light, ed. Stephen Benne Phillips
  (Rizzoli, 2005), © The Phillips Collection,
  p. 63. Courtesy of the artist.
Back cover Art: (top) Pablo Picasso, *Woman
  with a Book*, 1932. Oil on canvas,
  51¾ in. × 38½ in. The Norton Simon
  Foundation, Pasadena, CA, Estate of
  Robert Ellis Simon, 1969. © 2005 estate
  of Pablo Picasso/Artists Rights Society
  (ARS), New York.
  (bottom) Vincent van Gogh, *Vincent's Chair
  with Pipe*, 1888. Oil on canvas,
  36 in. × 28¾ in. National Gallery, London.
Printer/Binder: R. R. Donnelley/Harrisonburg
Cover Printer: Phoenix Color Corp.

Credits and acknowledgments borrowed from other sources and reproduced, with permission, in this textbook appear on appropriate page within text.

Pearson Education LTD.
Pearson Education, Canada, Ltd.
Pearson Education Australia PTY, Limited
Pearson Educación de Mexico, S.A. de C.V.
Pearson Education Singapore, Pte. Ltd.

Pearson Education—Japan
Pearson Education North Asia Ltd.
Pearson Education Malaysia, Pte. Ltd.
Pearson Education, Upper Saddle River,
  New Jersey

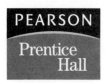

10 9 8 7 6 5 4 3 2 1
ISBN 10 020-564578-X
ISBN 13 978-020-564578-7

CONTENTS

Illustrations   viii

Preface   ix

Acknowledgments   xi

INTRODUCTION: Writing as Critical Thinking   1

1

**CHOOSING IMAGES: How to Select the Works
of Art You Plan to Write About**   9

Visiting Museums and Galleries,   9

Choosing Works of Art to Write About: Some Questions of Taste,   16

Writing Comparative Essays: Some Advantages,   18

Choosing Works from "The Museum without Walls,"   21

The Computer and "The Museum without Walls,"   23

Summary,   26

2

**USING VISUAL INFORMATION: What to Look For
and How to Describe What You See**   28

Considering the Subject Matter of the Work,   30

Describing the Formal Elements You Discover in the Work,   33

Line,   33

Shape and Space,   35

Light and Dark,   38

Color,   41

Other Elements,   45

Recognizing the Principles of Design,   52
Rhythm and Repetition,   52
Balance,   53
Proportion,   54
Scale,   55
Unity and Variety,   56

Considering Questions of Medium,   57

Beginning Your Essay By Describing the Work,   58

Asking Yourself about the Work of Art: A Summary,   62

Questions to Ask Before Writing About a Work of Art,   62

3

RESPONDING TO THE VERBAL FRAME: Where Else to Look for Help in Understanding What You See   64

Taking the Title and Label into Account,   64

Considering Informational Labels Accompanying the Work,   68

Consulting Artists' Statements and Exhibition Catalogues,   70

Discovering Other Helpful Material in the Library and Online,   71
Research Online,   72
Using the Library Catalog and Databases,   75
Using Art Dictionaries and Other Guides,   78

Considering the Work's Historical and Cultural Context,   79

Quoting and Documenting Your Sources,   86
Learning the Art of Quoting,   86
Acknowledging Your Sources,   87
Choosing Your Footnote Style,   88
Citing Internet Sources,   93

4

WORKING WITH WORDS AND IMAGES: The Process of Writing About What You See   95

Gathering Together What You Know,   95
Taking Notes in a Gallery or Museum,   95
Taking Notes As You Read,   96

Focusing Your Discussion,   98
Brainstorming and Mapping,   100
Using Prewriting As a Way to Begin,   101
Online Writing,   106

Creating a Finished Essay,   108
Organizing Your Essay: From Description to the Verbal Frame,   108
Developing an Argument or Thesis,   113

Revising and Editing, 115
A Revision Checklist, 116
Writing About Art: The Final Product, 117

Appendix
**A SHORT GUIDE TO USAGE AND STYLE: The Rules
and Principles of Good Writing 122**

1. Possessive Apostrophes, 123

2. Commas, 123

3. Comma Splices, 124

4. Run-on Sentences, 125

5. *That* and *Which*, 125

6. Titles, 125

7. Foreign Phrases, 126

8. Split Infinitives, 126

9. Sentence Fragments, 127

10. Colons, 127

11. Semicolons, 127

12. Dashes, 128

13. Parentheses, 129

14. Quotations, 129

15. Ellipses, 130

16. Dangling Modifiers, 131

17. Subject-Verb Agreement, 131

18. Pronoun Agreement, 132

19. Pronouns and Gender Issues, 132

20. Indefinite Antecedents (*it* and *this*), 132

21. Correlative Expressions, 133

22. Verb Tense Consistency, 134

23. Diction Consistency, 134

24. Concrete and Specific Language, 135

25. Frequently Misspelled Words, 135

Notes 137

Index 141

ILLUSTRATIONS

1. Andy Warhol, *Brillo Boxes*, 1970 (enlarged refabrication of 1964 project).
2. David Reed, *Judy's Bedroom*, from the installation *Two Bedrooms in San Francisco*, 1993/1996.
3. Carrie Mae Weems, *Coffee Pot*, 1988.
4. Richard Serra, *Tilted Arc*, 1981.
5. Richard Serra, *Tilted Arc*, 1981.
6. Frank Gehry, Guggenheim Museum Bilbao, 1997.
7. Richard Serra, *Snake*, 1994–97.
8. Charles Sheeler, *Bucks County Barn*, 1918.
9. Edward Hicks, *The Cornell Farm* (detail), 1848.
10. Gustave Courbet, *A Burial at Ornans*, 1849.
11. Pietro Perugino, *The Crucifixion with the Virgin, St John, Saint Jerome, and Saint Mary Magdalene* (central panel), c. 1485.
12. Carlo Crivelli, *The Crucifixion*, c. 1475.
13. Claude Monet, *Gare Saint-Lazare, Paris: The Arrival of a Train*, 1877.
14. Franz Kline, *Mahoning*, 1956.
15. Georgia O'Keeffe, *Alligator Pears in a Basket*, 1923.
16. Käthe Kollwitz, *The Downtrodden*, 1900.
17. Vincent van Gogh, *The Night Café*, 1888.
18. Phidias and workshop, *Three Goddesses*, c. 435 B.C.
19. Isamu Noguchi, Sculpture Garden, Isamu Noguchi Garden Museum, 1987.
20. Henri Cartier-Bresson, *Gare St. Lazare*, 1932.
21. Bill Viola, *Room for St. John of the Cross*, 1983.
22. Christo and Jeanne-Claude, *Wrapped Reichstag*, 1971–95.
23. Andreas Gursky, *Untitled V*, 1997.
24. Paul Cézanne, *Mont Sainte-Victoire*, 1885–87.
25. Paul Cézanne, *Mont Sainte-Victoire*, 1904–6.
26. Nikolai Buglaj, *Racial Optical Illusion*, 1997.
27. Shirin Neshat, *Rapture*, 1997.
28. Christo, *The Gates, Project for Central Park, New York City*, 2004.
29. Christo and Jeanne-Claude, *The Gates, Project for Central Park, New York City*, 1979–2005.
30. Walker Evans, *Washroom and Dining Area of Floyd Burroughs's Home, Hale County, Alabama*, 1936.
31. Jackson Pollock, *Full Fathom Five*, 1947.
32. Magical figure, *nikisi nkonde*, Kongo (Muserongo), Zaire, late nineteenth century.
33. Albrecht Dürer, *Draftsman Drawing a Reclining Nude*, from *The Art of Measurement*, c. 1527.
34. Kara Walker, *Insurrection! (Our Tools Were Rudimentary, Yet We Pressed On)*, installation view, 2000.
35. Roy Lichtenstein, *Brushstroke*, model completed 1996, fabricated and installed 2003.
36. Roy Lichtenstein, *Little Big Painting*, 1964.
37. Alexander Calder, *Two Discs*, 1965.
38. Francisco Goya, *The Countess of Chinchón*, 1800.
39. Jacques Louis David, *Portrait of Madame Trudaine*, 1791.

Front Cover: Sean Scully, *Vincent*, 2002.
Back cover Pablo Picasso, *Woman with Book*, 1932; Vincent van Gogh, *Vincent's Chair with Pipe*, 1888.

PREFACE

As a teacher of undergraduate courses in art appreciation and art history, I have always felt that one of the most important activities students engage in is writing. It is my conviction that the better, and the sooner, students write about what they see, the better they will see. To write about art is to engage in the best process I know for organizing—even recognizing—your thoughts and feelings about the visual world.

This book is addressed to you, the student of art. I hope that it will help you to write about art more effectively and thus teach you, through the process of writing, how to see works of art in more meaningful and lasting terms. Many of you are already effective writers, many of you may still lack the confidence you need to feel that you write well. If you are reading this book, you almost surely find the problem of writing about art a vexing one. If the visual arts expressed the same things in the same way as the verbal arts, then why would anyone bother to paint or sculpt or take photographs in the first place? Most people feel that images tend to "say" things that words can't. For them, being asked to write about art is like being asked to express the inexpressible.

Without denying the uniqueness of the visual experience, let me suggest that works of art are a form of address, directed at you, their audience. Like most forms of address, they demand a response. To write about a work of art is to respond in what for most of us is the most readily available means. To demonstrate the kinds of response a work of art might generate, I have written, in this book, about works of art that have excited me—and continue to excite me—and I have also included several responses to works of art written by my students. These essays were generated in my classes and, if they are not always the "best" imaginable response to a given assignment, they represent an effort on my part to choose the kind of writing that you can learn from best. For that reason as well, I have not generally used passages from renowned critics or historians to illustrate writing techniques. I have nothing against aspiring writers attempting to imitate the best practicing critics and historians, but imitation is difficult for many students and not, I believe, the most effective way to teach writing. The business of a book such as this is to build confidence, to give you a foundation upon which you can improve. Judging from the overwhelmingly positive student reception to this book, I can't help but think that good student writing is a more useful model than the stylistic subtleties of professionally wrought prose.

For this, the sixth edition of *Writing About Art*, I have made several changes. When this book was first published in 1989, the World Wide Web was still something of a dream. When the second edition of this book was published in 1995, I began my discussion on research methods as follows: "First, go to the card catalogue. It may or may not be an actual 'catalogue'—libraries are rapidly converting their catalogues to database formats, accessible at computer stations." Today, there may still be a few libraries that are not "online," but I don't know where they are. Although I sometimes think that the technology is changing as rapidly as I can write a sentence, in this edition, as in the last two, I have tried to address the changing environment of research and writing in art. Images are far more readily available. Databases are becoming increasingly sophisticated. The "blog" has become one of the most popular forms of writing on the Web. I have tried to give some idea of the increasingly rich resources available in the exploding world of the information highway.

Perhaps the most notable change, however, is the new Introduction, with its focus on writing as critical thinking. In the fourth edition of my art appreciation textbook, *A World of Art*, I began to treat the analysis and understanding of works of art as an exercise in critical thinking, an approach so popular among both teachers and students that many requested that I emphasize critical thinking in *Writing About Art* as well. In fact, much of what I wrote about critical thinking in *A World of Art* was already implicit in this book, and I believe that in making critical thinking the overt focus of discussion here, the book's arguments and suggestions have been strengthened considerably.

Finally, let me say that I hope this book convinces you that writing about art is a rewarding and pleasurable experience, an act of exploration and discovery in some ways comparable to the creative act itself. At the very least, this book should help you to write better exams and papers in your art appreciation and art history courses. In the end, I hope the book increases your confidence—and joy—in the process of writing itself.

Henry Sayre

ACKNOWLEDGMENTS

As I have said in every edition of this book since the beginning, the idea of writing this book began many years ago, when as a graduate student in American Literature at the University of Washington in Seattle, I taught freshman composition under the direction of William F. Irmscher, author of the famous Holt Guide. I continue to hope that something of the pleasure he took in teaching us to teach composition comes through in these pages.

Over the years at Prentice Hall, I have had the pleasure of working with many great editors, including my present editor, Amber Mackey. She has been terrifically supportive and encouraging in all of our work together, and I am extremely grateful. Thanks also to Amber's assistant, editor Alexandra Huggins, who keeps all the cogs turning. But I still owe most to Kevin Johnson, who first suggested this project, and especially to Norbert "Bud" Therien, one of the truly great art editors in the history of the business, who guided this book through its first four editions.

Finally, I want to thank all the faculty and students who over the years have written me with suggestions for minor and major revisions. You continue to help me make this book better. And so, once again, this book is for you.

INTRODUCTION
Writing as Critical Thinking

Over twenty-five years ago, philosopher and art critic Arthur C. Danto began to consider the question, What is it that makes something a work of art? It was his visit, in 1964, to a New York exhibition of Andy Warhol Brillo boxes that set him to wondering (Figure 1):

> I recall the philosophical intoxication that survived the aesthetic repugnance of his exhibition in 1964, at what was then the Stable Gallery on East 74th Street, where facsimiles of Brillo cartons were piled one upon the other, as though the gallery had been pressed into service as a warehouse for surplus scouring pads. . . . Some irrelevant negative mutterings aside, "Brillo Box" was instantly accepted as art; but the question became aggravated of why Warhol's Brillo boxes *were* works of art while their commonplace counterparts, in the back rooms of supermarkets throughout Christendom, were not.[1]

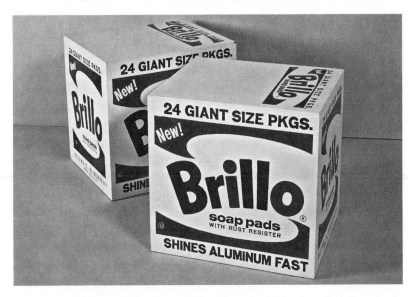

Figure 1   Andy Warhol, *Brillo Boxes*, 1970 (enlarged refabrication of 1964 project) Commercial silkscreen inks on industrially fabricated plywood box supports, each: 20 in. × 20 in. × 17 in. Allen Memorial Art Museum, Oberlin College, Ohio. Gift of John Coplans in memory of Ruth C. Roush, 1980. AMAM 1980.106.1–2. © 2009 The Andy Warhol Foundation for the Visual Arts/Artists Rights Society (ARS), NY

Once posed, the question remained at the forefront of Danto's writing for decades. In 1995, for instance, when he delivered the A. W. Mellon Lectures in the Fine Arts at Princeton University, he argued that works such as Warhol's *Brillo Boxes* announced that "art," as the Western world had conceived of it since the Renaissance, no longer existed. This is not to say that art per se was dead—to the contrary, Danto found contemporary art to be "extremely vigorous," showing "no sign whatever of internal exhaustion"[2]— but rather that our traditional way of understanding art no longer applied.

This is not the place to rehearse Danto's thesis. It is extremely intricate and complex, and it has, after all, preoccupied him for over a quarter of a century. But his "philosophical intoxication" with his subject is instructive. Danto asked himself a question that he could not easily answer. It was such a good question that it has resulted in literally hundreds of pages of what many people consider to be some of the best art writing of the last fifty years.

This, then, is the first principle of this book: Good writing begins with good questions. To ask a good question is, in turn, a product of the process of questioning, exploration, trial and error, revision, and discovery that we call critical thinking.

One of the greatest benefits of studying art is that it teaches you to think critically. Art objects are generally "mute." They cannot explain themselves to you, but that does not mean that their meaning is "hidden" or elusive. They contain information—all kinds of information—that can help you explain and understand them if you approach them through the critical thinking process.

Critical thinking is first and foremost a matter of putting yourself in a *questioning* frame of mind. Our culture is increasingly dominated by images, and all students today must learn to see and interpret the visual world around them. As you question what you see, as you actively engage the world of art—and not just passively "receive" its images, like some television set—you will find that you are at once critical and self-critical. You will see better and understand more—about both the work of art and yourself.

The last several editions of the art appreciation textbook *A World of Art* have included a Student Toolkit in which we have outlined seven steps to thinking critically about art. These steps have proven so useful to so many students that it seemed logical to begin this book with them as well.

1. *Identify the artist's decisions and choices and question why those decisions and choices were made.*
   Begin by recognizing that, in making works of art, artists inevitably make certain decisions and choices—What color should I make this

area? Should my line be wide or narrow, straight or curved? Will I look up at my subject or down on it? Will I depict it realistically or not? What medium should I use to make this object? And so on. Identify these choices. Then ask yourself why these choices were made. Remember, although most artists work somewhat intuitively, every artist has the opportunity to revise or redo each work, each gesture. You can be sure that what you are seeing in a work of art is an intentional effect.

2. *Ask more questions. Be curious.*

Asking yourself why the artist's choices were made is just the first set of questions to pose. You need to consider the work's title: what does it tell you about the piece? Is there any written material accompanying the work? Is the work informed by the context in which you encounter it— by other works around it, or, in the case of sculpture for instance, by its location? Is there anything you learn about the artist that is helpful?

3. *Describe the object.*

By carefully describing the object—both its subject matter and how its subject matter is formally realized—you can discover much about the artist's intentions. Pay careful attention to how one part of the work relates to the others.

4. *Question your assumptions.*

Question, particularly, any initial dislike you might have for a given work of art. Remember that if you are seeing the work in a book, museum, or gallery, then someone likes it. Ask yourself why. Often you'll talk yourself into liking it too. But also examine the work itself to see if it contains any biases or prejudices. It matters, for instance, in Renaissance church architecture whether the church is designed for Protestants or Catholics.

5. *Avoid an emotional response.*

Art objects are supposed to stir up your feelings, but your emotions can sometimes get in the way of clear thinking. Analyze your own emotions. Determine what about the work set them off, and ask yourself if this wasn't the artist's very intention.

6. *Don't oversimplify or misrepresent the art object.*

Art objects are complex by their nature. To think critically about an art object is to look beyond the obvious. Thinking critically about the work of art always involves walking the line between the work's susceptibility to interpretation and its integrity, or its resistance to arbitrary and capricious readings. Be sure your reading of a work of art is complete enough (that it recognizes the full range of possible meanings the work might possess), and, at the same time, that it doesn't violate or misrepresent the work.

7. *Tolerate uncertainty.*

Remember that critical thinking is an exercise in discovery, that it is designed to uncover possibilities, not necessarily certain truths. It is a process of questioning; asking good questions is sometimes more important than arriving at "right" answers. There may, in fact, be no "right" answers.

The process of writing about art, then, begins with recognizing that certain decisions have been made and wondering why. Chapter 1, "Choosing Images," is about how to put yourself in the best position to recognize these decisions. Viewing a work of art and writing about it involves, of course, some initial questioning on your own part. You have to ask yourself, "Among all the possible images for me to write about in the museum or gallery, or in a book, which is the work of art I can write about most effectively?" Then, having made an intelligent choice of your own, you can begin to determine what meaningful choices the artist has made.

Arthur Danto is a master at choosing images that successfully reflect the questions that he poses to himself about the nature of art. His 1995 book *Art after the End of Art* opens with a film still from Alfred Hitchcock's classic 1958 movie *Vertigo*. But the image is no mere film still. The painter David Reed has altered it by placing one of his own abstract paintings, *#328* of 1990, on the wall behind the actress Kim Novak, who plays Judy, the film's lead female character. Reed subsequently transferred the still to a video loop, which played continuously on a television in an installation consisting of the television monitor, a bed, and above the bed the actual painting, *#328* (Figure 2). Why is it, Danto wondered, that an artist so thoroughly dedicated to painting in its own right should choose to put his painting in such a context?

The choice, Danto says, reflects at least two of Reed's obsessions:

> He is enough obsessed with *Vertigo* that he once made a pilgrimage to all the remaining sites in San Francisco that appear in Hitchcock's film. . . . The other obsession is with the idea of what he terms "bedroom painting." The expression was used by his mentor, Nicholas Wilder, in connection with the paintings of John McLaughlin. Buyers of those paintings would initially hang them in one of the more public spaces of the home, but in time, Wilder said, "They would move the painting to their bedroom where they could live with it more intimately." Reed responded as if to a revelation: "My ambition in life was to be a bedroom painter." The modified video implies that Judy lives intimately with

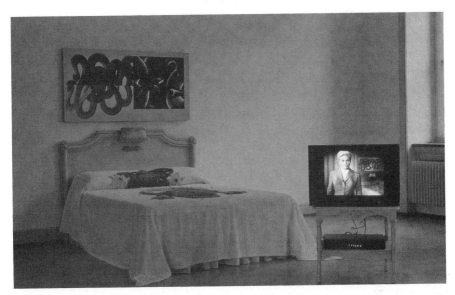

Figure 2   David Reed, *Judy's Bedroom*, from *Two Bedrooms in San Francisco*, 1993/1996. Oil on canvas, bed, and television set, variable dimensions. Courtesy Max Protetch Gallery. 1992. Ensenble. Featuring painting #328, 1990-93. Installation *You look good in blue*. Kunstmuseum St. Gallen, 2001. Photo: Kunstmuseum St. Gallen/ Stefan Rohner

> *#328*, and by putting *#328* in the viewer's space with a bed . . . Reed directs the viewer how to relate to *#328* should he or she happen to acquire it, or any painting by Reed.[3]

For Danto, Reed's installation exemplifies "contemporary artistic practice . . . a practice in which painters no longer hesitate to situate their paintings by means of devices which belong to altogether different media—sculpture, video, film, installation, and the like."[4] Danto's self-imposed challenge in *Art after the End of Art* was to discover why contemporary artists no longer conceived of their work as "pure," as individual objects to be considered in their own terms without recourse to the world around them. Why is it, he wonders, that in contemporary art "anything goes?"[5]

As Danto asks this question, he describes the multiple aspects of David Reed's work—not the installation alone, but the "pure painting" that Reed incorporates into his installation, with its broad, swirling brush-strokes at the left and its square of darkly lit folds of black at the right. It is, of course, the tension between the purity of Reed's painting and the banality of the scene in which Reed frames it that most fascinates Danto.

And he begins his book by describing the elements at play in Reed's work. You will need to describe the visual elements and media at play in whatever works you choose to write about as well. Chapter 2, "Using Visual Information," is a summary of the visual elements from which an artist might choose, the principles of composition that an artist might use to organize a work (or, perhaps, intentionally violate), and the various media an artist might choose to employ or combine. The intention of the chapter is to help you recognize what sorts of visual information might be important for you to write about, but if you find you need more help or further elaboration, you should consult one of the many discussions of the visual elements that are widely available in art appreciation texts, including my own *A World of Art*.

In Chapter 3, "Responding to the Verbal Frame," the problem of words and their relation to the image is addressed. All images are surrounded by words—in their titles, in accompanying exhibition materials, in critical and art historical discussions. Some works of art even contain words, as does, for instance, Carrie Mae Weems's photograph of a common coffee pot (Figure 3). But most works of art are surrounded by words beyond the frame itself. Depending upon the nature of the essay you have to write, you may or may not want to consult secondary sources such as critical commentaries or monographs for help in understanding the image. Some of this verbal material, however, is essential, and, in one way or another, it all can help you begin to think about your own verbal approach to the work of art.

Chapter 4, "Working with Words and Images," is about the crucial activity of writing itself. One of the first things you will discover, if you don't already know it, is that there is a slippage or gap between the image and its meaning. Take, for instance, Carrie Mae Weems's photograph. Visually, it's just a coffee pot, or more precisely, a photograph entitled *Coffee Pot*. That said, already, we've slipped away from the object itself, since this coffee pot has been acted upon, photographed, selected, "posed," if you will, arranged, framed, lit, and most of all, assimilated into the world of Carrie Mae Weems, a world much more fully defined by the text that accompanies it.

Weems's image/texts are strategies of opposition. Her parents, in *Coffee Pot*, are "sipping like white folks on t.v." Drinking coffee makes them look white to their daughter, and yet they warn her that drinking coffee will "make you black." The seemingly "straight" photograph, which seems merely to document the way things are, is juxtaposed to Weems's first-person narration, which possesses its own authority of an authentic voice, a voice that tells us what this coffee pot means to Weems. If the

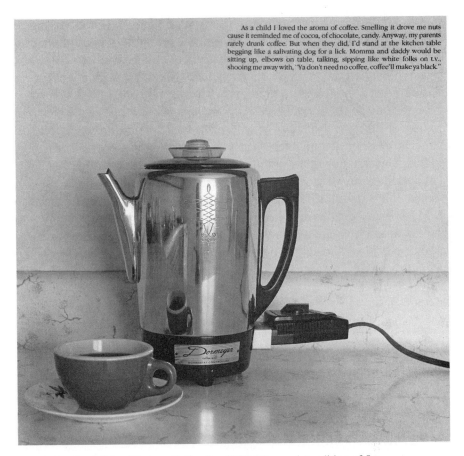

As a child I loved the aroma of coffee. Smelling it drove me nuts cause it reminded me of cocoa, of chocolate, candy. Anyway, my parents rarely drunk coffee. But when they did, I'd stand at the kitchen table begging like a salivating dog for a lick. Momma and daddy would be sitting up, elbows on table, talking, sipping like white folks on t.v., shooing me away with, "Ya don't need no coffee, coffee'll make ya black."

Figure 3   Carrie Mae Weems, *Coffee Pot*, 1988. Silver print, edition of 5, 14½ in. × 14½ in. Courtesy P.P.O.W., Inc. New York.

photograph attests that the coffee pot is, or was at one time, real, Weems's narration describes its greater reality. As we move from image to text, from one sense to another, that is, from the sight of the coffee pot to its aroma, we move from the "truth" of photography to the fiction of Weems's story, from the language of black-and-white photography to the realities of being black and white in America.

Weems's narrative seems to open up the image to the possibilities of meaning, but especially in the first stages of writing, your own attempts to put words to images will often seem *reductive*. While whatever you have to say might well be true, you will likely feel that it is true only to a degree. Most images are more ambiguous than you will at first be willing to admit. You will want to pin the image down, understand it, and you will tend to think that understanding is itself unambiguous. But if you agree that one of the primary reasons to write about art is to *interpret* the meaning of the images it presents, and if you reflect on the word *interpretation* for a moment, you can see that almost by definition a work's meaning is never single; it is always open to discussion and debate.

Writing about works of art will, finally, teach you one of the most important of all critical habits—it will teach you to question what you see. Most professors are not necessarily interested in your discovering the "right" interpretation of a work of art—they recognize a certain "openness" and amplitude in all works of art. They are, however, interested in seeing you ask hard questions about the work itself and about your responses to it. My primary goal as an educator—and I share this goal with many others—is to teach you to actively engage your world. We all want you to be at once a critical and self-critical thinker. Writing about art is one way to begin this larger process. The skills you develop will be, I promise, applicable to whatever endeavor you choose to pursue in your life.

1

CHOOSING IMAGES
How to Select the Works of Art
You Plan to Write About

Unless your professor assigns specific works of art for you to write about, one of the most difficult tasks you face is selecting an appropriate subject, one that is accessible and manageable, and yet challenging enough to provoke interesting thought and writing. This chapter is designed to help you choose an appropriate topic from the outset. One of the first things you need to take into consideration is the context in which you approach the work.

VISITING MUSEUMS AND GALLERIES

When you enter a museum, how do you feel, and do your feelings affect the way you see? This is not so much to ask whether you feel happy or sad, bored or confused—though your mood and temperament can obviously affect your perception of things—but whether the museum itself reminds you of a church or a library, a lecture hall or a department store. In the late 1960s, two French scholars surveyed a cross-section of the French population and discovered that 66 percent of all manual workers, 45 percent of all skilled and blue-collar workers, and 30.5 percent of professionals and upper-level managers most closely associated museums with churches. A large group of the skilled and white-collar workers—34 percent—felt that the museum was most analogous to the library. Of the professionals and managers, 28 percent likened the museum to the library. Only small percentages of each group felt that they were like lecture halls or department stores. But a large number of professionals, nearly 20 percent, felt that a museum was like none of these other institutions. A museum, they must have felt, is most like itself.[1]

These figures can be interpreted in any number of useful and interesting ways, but my point is a simple one: For most people, the museum possesses an aura, a mystique, that literally transforms the work of art. The museum removes art from the context of everyday life. Everywhere there are signs—"Please Do Not Touch the Works of Art"—that imply to

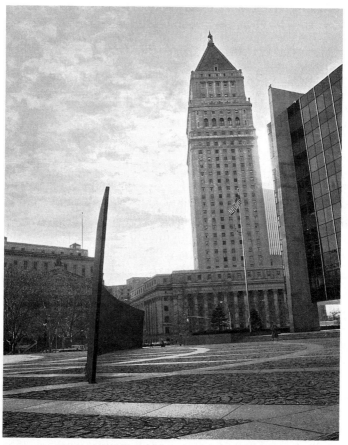

Figure 4   Richard Serra, *Tilted Arc*, 1981. Cor-Ten steel, 12 ft. × 120 ft. × 2½ in. Installed Federal Plaza, New York City. Destroyed by the U. S. Government, 3/15/89. © 2006 Richard Serra/ Artists Rights Society (ARS), New York/ADAGP, Paris. Getty Images

many people not only the "purity" and "sanctity" of art itself, but by extension their own relative corruption. Like the library, the museum also demands their *silent* contemplation and study of its objects. It is the kind of space in which people feel compelled to whisper, reverently, and in which parents feel obliged to collar their children, put them on their best behavior, and demand their submissive attention.

Context plays a large role in determining the way in which we see. Consider the sculpture by Richard Serra entitled *Tilted Arc*, which for eight years, from 1981 to 1989, was installed in the plaza in front of the Jacob R. Javits Federal Building in Lower Manhattan, home of the General Services Administration (Figures 4 and 5). During its life span, the piece dominated the space, standing over twelve feet high, leaning slightly inward as if about to fall, forcing people to walk around it, and blocking the natural sight lines implied by the plaza's stonework in a manner that was purposefully confrontational. As Serra explained, "It is necessary to work in opposition to the constraints of the context, so that the work cannot be read as an affirmation of questionable ideologies and political power."[2] Though many people appreciated its aggressive presence, many others did not. William Diamond, Regional Administrator of the General Services Administration, in March 1985 began lobbying to have it removed. Of the approximately 12,000 employees working in the complex, 3,791 signed a petition supporting Diamond's efforts. But nearly as

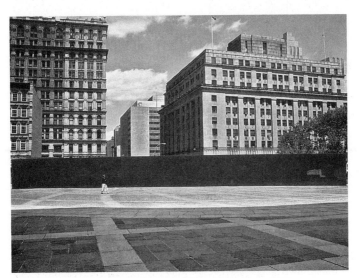

Figure 5   Richard Serra, *Tilted Arc*, 1981. Cor-Ten steel,
12 ft. × 120 ft. × 2½ in. Installed Federal Plaza, New York City.
Destroyed by the U. S. Government, 3/15/89. © 2006 Richard Serra/
Artists Rights Society (ARS), New York/ADAGP, Paris. © Corbis.

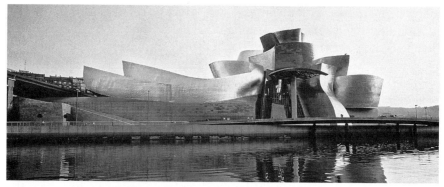

Figure 6   Frank Gehry, Solomon R. Guggenheim Museum Bilbao, Bilbao, Spain, 1997. © FMGB Guggenheim Bilbao Museoa, 2005. Photographer Erika Barahona Ede.

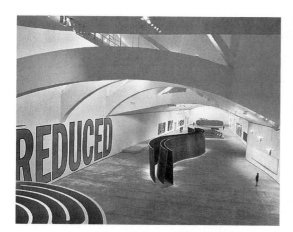

Figure 7   Richard Serra, *Snake*, 1994–97. Interior view of Guggenheim Museum Bilbao, Boat Gallery. © FMGB Guggenheim bilbao Museoa, 2005. Photographer Erika Barahona Ede.

many—3,763—signed a petition to save it. At a hearing in March 1985 convened to consider its removal, one security guard testified that she considered it a "blast wall":

> The *Arc* is what I consider to be a security hazard or a disadvantage. My main contention is that it presents a blast wall effect. . . . It's 120 feet long, 12 feet high, and it's angled in a direction toward both federal buildings, 1 Federal Plaza and 26 Federal Plaza. The front curvature of the design is comparable to devices which are used by bomb experts to vent explosive forces. The purpose of these . . . bomb devices is to vent explosions upward. This one could vent an explosion both upward and in an angle toward both buildings. . . . It would, of course, take a larger bomb than [those] which have been previously used to destroy enough for their purposes; but it is possible, and lately we are expecting the worst in the federal sector.[3]

The security guard's "reading" of *Tilted Arc* attributes to Serra's work a function that is completely alien to his artistic intentions, even if, in the context of more recent history—the Oklahoma City bombing was still ten years away when this security guard testified—it makes a certain perverse sense. Out in the plaza, its status as art (and not a "blast wall") was not entirely clear.

On the night of March 15, 1989, against Serra's vehement protests and after he had filed a lawsuit seeking to block its removal, the sculpture was dismantled and its parts stored in a Brooklyn warehouse. It has subsequently been destroyed—something of a formality from Serra's point of view, since, as he put it, "To remove the *Tilted Arc* . . . is to destroy it."[4] Its art depended on its relation to its site, and the art of Serra's work is much more apparent in a work created for more obviously artworld sites, such as the Solomon R. Guggenheim Museum in Bilbao, Spain, designed by architect Frank Gehry (Figure 6). Covered in titanium, sweeping along the Bilbao waterfront in giant arcs and curves, Gehry's museum is a remarkably contemporary piece of design. Its lines are so reminiscent of Serra's work that it seemed natural to invite Serra to create a sculpture for the new museum's largest space, the 450-foot-long, 80-foot-wide "Boat Gallery"—a space large enough to house two Boeing 747s. Serra responded with a double, tilted, curving piece called *Snake* (Figure 7). *Snake* is itself so large that it had to be installed before the building was completed, and it can never be removed.

The power of Serra's example lies in the fact that it forces us to recognize that the aesthetic dimension of a thing might be more a function of where we see it than of any quality inherent in the thing itself—or, put another way, in the right context, we more readily recognize the work's aesthetic qualities. In the same manner, the walls, the frames that surround paintings, and other works in a given gallery space influence the ways in which we see works of art. One of the best analyses of this situation can be found in a series of essays by Brian O'Doherty, originally written for *Artforum* in the mid-1970s, entitled "Inside the White Cube." As O'Doherty says,

> The ideal gallery . . . subtracts from the artwork all the cues that interfere with the fact that it is "art." The work is isolated from everything that would detract from [it]. . . . The outside world must not come in, so windows are usually sealed off. Walls are painted white. The wooden floor is polished so that you click along clinically or carpeted so that you pad soundlessly, resting the feet while the eyes have at the wall. The art is free, as the saying used to go, "to take on its own life."[5]

The art is anything but free, however, and this ambiguity, which is perhaps inevitable, repeats itself in various forms throughout our experience of it. For although the work of art is technically isolated from things that would interfere with our appreciation of it for its own sake and in its own terms, it perpetually encounters a force "from the outside," one might say, a force that is always violating its sanctity. It is always meeting the enemy face to face—and the enemy is us.

We carry all manner of baggage with us when we see works of art; it may include a downright distaste for the particular work of art we happen to be looking at, and, as the example of the security guard looking at Serra's *Tilted Arc* demonstrates, what we carry not only affects what we see but how well we see it. Seeing art, then, as much as it is a critical operation, is a self-critical one as well. It involves, absolutely, examining our own prejudices and preconceptions. If the work of art seems distant from us, isolated there on the wall, that is so because, in a certain sense, it needs that protection. Museum histories are rife with examples of the mutilation of works of art. But the work of art needs also to rise above whatever ignorance or misunderstanding we might initially bring to it—even if we aren't about to abuse it physically. It needs to demand our respect. The history of modern art is in some ways the history of the public's misapprehension and disapprobation of art it would eventually come to admire and love. Almost everyone today likes Impressionist painting. Yet when it first appeared in France in the 1870s, it was thought laughable, even scandalous. In his 1886 novel, *The Masterpiece*, Emile Zola provides a fictionalized account of the crowd's reaction to an Impressionist painting that more or less summarizes the way in which much of the work of his friends and contemporaries—Manet, Cézanne, Monet, Sisley—was initially received:

> It was one long-drawn-out explosion of laughter, rising in intensity to hysteria. As soon as they reached the doorway, he saw visitors' faces expand into anticipated mirth, their eyes narrow, their mouths broaden into a grin, and from every side came tempestuous puffings and blowings from fat men, rusty, grating whimperings from thin ones, and, dominating all the rest, high-pitched, fluty giggles from the women. A group of young men on the opposite side of the room were writhing as if their ribs were being tickled. One woman had collapsed on to a bench, her knees pressed tightly together, gasping, struggling to regain her breath behind her handkerchief. . . . The ones who did not laugh lost their tempers, taking the overall blueness [of the picture], Claude's original way of rendering the effect of daylight, as an insult to their intelligence. It was an outrage and should be stopped, according to elderly gentlemen who brandished their walking sticks in indignation. One very serious individual, as he stalked away in anger, was heard announcing to his wife that he had no use for bad jokes. . . . It was beginning to look like a riot. More and more people kept forcing their way up to the picture, and as the heat grew more intense faces grew more and more purple.[6]

Context is playing a large part in determining the reaction of this crowd. The picture they are outraged by describes nature—the effects of daylight—in what is, to them, a new way. It is unlike anything else in their experience. And it is unlike anything else around it. It is hanging, further-more, in what was known as the Salon des Refusés, an exhibition of all the works that were submitted to the main Salon but refused acceptance by the French Academy. It is, from the point of view of the crowd, the most scan-dalously bad painting in an exhibition of officially bad paintings.

It is perhaps fair to say that one reason we have so little trouble our-selves in seeing paintings such as the one described by Zola as works of great beauty, rather than as objects of derision, is that we are used to see-ing a great many of them, together, in the large gallery devoted to Impres-sionist painting in the Metropolitan Museum, for instance, or on the top floor of the Musée d'Orsay in Paris. Here, seen as a group, the paintings tend to inform one another. We can see for ourselves, in a series of Monet grainstacks, how at different times of day, in different seasons of the year, and in different weather, the same scene can dramatically alter in effect. Or we can witness the logical growth of Cézanne's ideas about composi-tion if we compare an early rendering of a particular motif, such as his *Mont Sainte-Victoire* of 1885–87 (Figure 24), discussed in Chapter 2, with a later version of the same scene (Figure 25).

One of the primary functions of museums is to provide just this sort of educational experience, to allow us to see *in context* works of art that in isolation might appear extravagant or ill-considered or even badly execut-ed. (And, on the other hand, they avoid grouping works together which ap-parently have nothing in common.) In commercial galleries, which after all are in the business of selling the works of art they display, the sense of unity and coherence is most readily apparent. The so-called "one-person" show, the staple of the gallery system, almost guarantees a coherent visu-al effect, and galleries themselves are often known by the particular "look" or style that they champion. A sense of unity can be achieved in any num-ber of ways, however, particularly in the larger context of the museum, where collections are sometimes wildly various and the potential for chaos is markedly greater. Commonly, in museums, works of art are grouped by artist (all the Monets in a single room), by school or group (the Cubists, for instance, in one room, the Futurists in the next), by theme (landscapes or portraits), by nationality and/or historical period (nineteenth-century British painting or seventeenth-century Dutch), by some critical theory, or by some combination of these ("Nineteenth-Century British Landscape," for instance, or "American Abstraction: Its Roots and Legacy").

Curators also often guarantee the continued movement of people through the museum by limiting the number of important or "star" works in any given space. The attention of the visitor is drawn to such works most often by positioning and lighting. When a particularly large painting occupies a wall, the other works in the room will almost always be smaller, and might even be drawings or sketches. A relatively small but important painting might be sumptuously framed, or hung by itself on a wall, perhaps accompanied by especially elaborate explanatory material.

The museum, in other words, is addressed to *you*. It wants to make art available to you, and it wants you to gather, from your experience, a greater understanding of and appreciation for what you've seen. Although the work of art, and the museum itself, might possess a certain aura of religiosity or sanctity, if we grant the art the respect that is its due, we are free to enter into a dialogue with it, for, like the museum as a whole, each individual work is addressed to its audience, individually and collectively. If you do not allow yourself to be intimidated by the museum, and if you recognize the ways in which your own responses are being manipulated— sometimes to great advantage—by the museum itself, this dialogue can be particularly interesting and worthwhile.

CHOOSING WORKS OF ART TO WRITE ABOUT: SOME QUESTIONS OF TASTE

One of the best ways to think of the task before you when you are asked to write about art is to approach it as a kind of dialogue between you and the work. It is your business, when you write about art, to record this dialogue. But there are dialogues and dialogues. You want to avoid having your dialogue turn into a *diatribe*. Therefore, the first rule of thumb is to avoid, if at all possible, writing about something you simply don't like or don't understand (often these are the same thing).

All too often, when we are confronted by things we do not understand, we react to them in the way that Zola's crowd reacted to the painting in *The Masterpiece*. We are all interested in reading why an authoritative critic dislikes a given work, but we risk appearing uninformed, even boorish, when we criticize what we don't understand. I have received, for instance, many a paper that pointed out how Manet or Picasso is a "bad" painter because, the argument goes, neither one "obviously" understands the laws of perspective. Of course, they *do* understand the laws of perspective but have chosen to violate those laws in order, among other things, to assert their independence from both traditional painting itself and conventional attitudes about the representational functions of painting. Such papers show not only that the writers are themselves traditional and conventional (not in itself particularly damning), but, more important, that they don't understand the paintings they are writing about.

You are entitled to your opinion. However, you should recognize the limitations of your opinion, and you should also recognize that in all likelihood your audience—namely your professor—is probably better informed on the subject than you are. This is not to say that you have to force yourself somehow to like all or even any of the works in a museum, or gallery, or in your text. But it is important that you recognize that someone, someone with a greater degree of expertise than yourself, thinks enough of them to have selected them, and you need to respect their choice. It is your business not only to enter into a dialogue with the work of art, but to have a *respectful* dialogue, one that tries to account for the presence of the work in the museum itself. In other words, it is a good tactic to neutralize, as much as possible, your own opinions and to account instead for the opinions of others. Say to yourself, "Someone likes this. Why? What's interesting about it?" Quite often you'll find that in accounting for the interest of others, you will become interested yourself.

Sometimes you might find yourself able to write about a work that you're sure you understand completely. For instance, I often give beginning students the opportunity to visit any gallery they choose and to write about any work they want. A great many gravitate toward landscapes that remind them of home or—the example is admittedly trite, but it is an actual one—a still life of daisies named *First Love*. The problem is that such works are often so accessible and so rudimentary in their appeal, that once you've said, "It reminds me of home," or "It reminds me of my boyfriend, who is always buying me flowers," there isn't much left to say. It's certainly not wrong to like images of this kind, but it is important to recognize that, whatever their emotional appeal, they often lack the kind of intellectual richness that other kinds of art possess. Their attraction, furthermore, might be purely personal and may be of little or no interest to anyone but you. At the very least, recognize that there may not be sufficient complexity in them to sustain an interesting essay.

All this implies that the best works of art to write about usually possess a reasonable *complexity*, that they *challenge* you intellectually, and that they sustain a high level of *interest* on a plane other than the purely personal. In my own writing, I have usually found that the best pieces I have done have resulted not from my attempt to explain what I already know to an "unknowing" audience, but from my attempts to engage a work that I find in some way powerful even as I am unable, at first, to articulate just what the sources of that power might be. Writing then becomes a kind of *exploration*. This leads in turn to better writing, because the sense of mystery, excitement, and discovery involved in the process of exploration is never lost.

WRITING COMPARATIVE ESSAYS: SOME ADVANTAGES

Art history is, by its very nature, a comparative process, and most works of art can be usefully thought of as dialogues with other works of art. As a result, it is often beneficial to write about several, since, in the process of comparing one work to another *related* work—and the two parts of a comparison should be related in some meaningful way—new ideas and perceptions about the work in question generally reveal themselves to the writer. Even if you are concentrating on a single work, comparing it to another can often shed light on a particular quality or effect that would otherwise be difficult to define or clarify.

Consider Charles Sheeler's *Bucks County Barn* (Figure 8), painted in 1918 when Sheeler was living in a Quaker house built in 1768 at the edge of Doylestown, Bucks County, Pennsylvania. It is generally assumed that this painting was executed under the influence of the new modern styles of art, particularly the Cubism of painters like Pablo Picasso and Georges Braque, and many interesting comparisons can be drawn between Sheeler's painting and Cubist work. By outlining the similarities between the two, one can begin to assess the impact of French Cubism on American art. Like the Cubist painter, Sheeler delineates the object in its most reduced

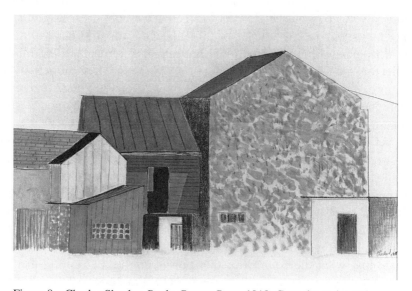

Figure 8   Charles Sheeler, *Bucks County Barn*, 1918. Gouache and conté crayon, 16⅛ in. × 22⅛ in. Columbus Museum of Art, Ohio. Gift of Ferdinand Howald.

form, relies on the differentiation of materials and surface textures for his visual effects, and emphasizes the two-dimensional surface of his canvas, flattening the scene in order to avoid creating an illusionistic three-dimensional space.

That said, there is something altogether American about Sheeler's work, something that exists outside the vocabulary of Cubist painting. In Milton W. Brown's classical account, outlined in his *American Painting: From the Armory Show to the Depression*, the "Americanness" of Sheeler's style is attributable to the vocabulary of "machine production and mechanical precision" that was so much a part of the American industrial age.[7] But consider a detail from a painting of another Bucks County barn, *The Cornell Farm*, painted by the untrained American artist Edward Hicks in 1848 (Figure 9). Just as Sheeler's work does, Hicks's painting emphasizes structural simplicity, textural surface, and especially two-dimensionality, though this latter is probably, in Hicks's work, more a matter of unskilled perspectival rendering than a question of intentional flattening. Since Sheeler was, in 1918, living in the same region where Hicks had originally painted, and since he was, furthermore, deeply committed to collecting the region's antiques and artifacts, particularly of Shaker origin, it is possible to see *Bucks County Barn* not so much as the expression of the new modern styles of painting such as Cubism but as evidence that

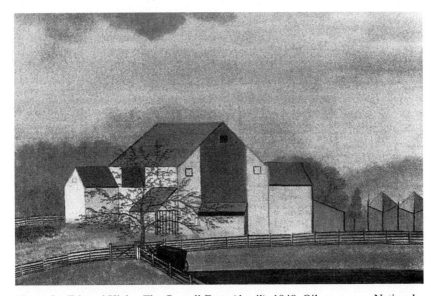

Figure 9   Edward Hicks, *The Cornell Farm* (detail), 1848. Oil on canvas. National Gallery of Art, Washington D.C. Gift of Edgar William and Bernice Chrysler Garbisch. © Board of Trustees, National Gallery of Art.

those styles had been anticipated in the native expressions of American art. It is as if Edward Hicks, the quintessential native-born and self-taught American painter, was, in 1848, a proto-Cubist. It is, in fact, possible to argue that Sheeler's work is not so much influenced by Cubism as it is willing to grant the validity of Cubism's way of seeing. The example of Hicks in a sense authorizes Sheeler's later Cubist idiom.[8]

It should be obvious that this understanding of the "Americanness" of Sheeler's painting results from comparing it to Hicks's earlier work. Comparative essays are the basis of art history because, in fact, it is through the comparative essay that art history is constructed. If we think for a moment about why the discipline should be so dependent on the form, the comparative essay's usefulness becomes much clearer.

How, we begin by asking, do art historians understand the development of a single painter? They look at early work by that painter and compare it to later works. They see, from one work to the next, a development, or a progress. They can see in the later work its roots in the earlier work. They see things in the earlier work that assume an importance they might otherwise not have if it were not for the fact that these relatively minor elements become major elements later on. Indeed, the connoisseurship of art, especially in its concern with attributing and authenticating works, is completely dependent on such comparative procedures.

These same procedures can easily be applied to the study of whole periods in the history of art as well, so that it becomes possible to trace, for instance, the development of a Baroque style, or of landscape in nineteenth-century American art. In each case, the art historian is tracing the progress of a style or approach to representation as it develops, as it increases in sophistication and complexity. An important assumption is at work here. The assumption is that a later work is more sophisticated than an earlier work, that there is a progress toward increasing complexity. Given this assumption, how would you write an essay comparing an early work by a given painter to a later one, or an early Baroque painting to a later one? You would develop a simple thesis: that the later work grows out of and depends upon certain features found in the earlier work, and, further, that the later work subsumes the earlier work and takes the problems or themes that it deals with to a new level, arriving at a new synthesis of some kind. This is precisely the way in which the argument above concerning Sheeler's debt to Hicks was developed.

Comparative essays are also used to explain change—the change for instance from the High Renaissance style of Michelangelo to his later Mannerist work, or the change in Picasso's work from his Blue Period to his Cubist painting, or from Neoclassicism to Romanticism. Here we begin with two radically different works or styles of art that seem to have nothing in common. The task is to explain why the characteristic elements of the first work have been abandoned for the second. The project is still historical—the later work abandons the principles of the earlier work, and you are asking *why*. Your thesis, in this case, is your explanation of the change. You are comparing the two works in order to explain this change.

Often in a comparative essay, you are engaged in both these approaches. On the one hand, you see certain kinds of continuity. On the other, you see certain kinds of change. Those two words—*continuity* and *change*—are the basis of most comparative essays.

When choosing what to write about, always consider what advantages for you there might be in a comparative approach, and then ask yourself these two questions: What changes from piece to piece? What stays the same? And then you must decide what all this means. What does this continuity or change tell us? What do we learn from the comparison? (If we learn nothing, then the comparison is not worth making, and you had better look for something else to write about.)

CHOOSING WORKS FROM "THE MUSEUM WITHOUT WALLS"

Writing about works of art seen in person has many advantages over writing about works one has seen only in books, but very often one has no choice. There is no substitute, for instance, for actually having walked around Richard Serra's *Tilted Arc*. Photographs do it little justice. Serra himself is acutely aware of this:

> If you reduce sculpture to the flat plane of the photograph, you're passing on only a residue of your concerns. You're denying the temporal experience of the work. You're not only reducing the sculpture to a different scale for the purposes of consumption, but you're denying the real content of the work. At least with most sculpture, the experience of the work is inseparable from the place in which the work resides. Apart from that condition, any experience of the work is a deception.[9]

Similarly, Gustave Courbet's giant canvas, *A Burial at Ornans* (Figure 10), in the Musée d'Orsay, must be seen in person to be fully appreciated. Even though, in the harsh light of this particular museum, many of the details readily apparent in reproduction are virtually lost, the scale of this massive painting, which hangs over us like the rocks of Ornans in its background, can be experienced only firsthand. It is this scale, together with the tension one feels between the monumentality of the literal canvas and the ordinariness of the scene depicted, that provides one of the most important insights into the painting of Courbet and its influence on modern art.

But most of us are condemned to what the French writer and novelist André Malraux called, somewhat more optimistically, "the museum without walls." What, Malraux asks, had the average expert on art, let alone the average citizen with an interest in art, actually *seen* in the nineteenth century?

> Two or three of the great museums, and photographs, engravings, or copies of a handful of the masterpieces of European art. . . . In the art knowledge of those days there existed an area of ambiguity: comparison of a picture in the Louvre with another in Madrid, in Florence, or in Rome was a comparison of a present vision with a memory. . . . Today, an art student can examine color reproductions of most of the world's great paintings and discover for himself a host of secondary works, as well as the archaic arts, the great epochs of Indian, Chinese, Japanese, and primitive and "folk" art. How many statues could be seen in reproduction in 1850? . . . A museum without walls has opened to us, and it will carry infinitely farther that limited revelation of the world of art which the real museums offer us within their walls.[10]

There are, as Malraux points out, some real advantages in having so many reproductions available on our coffee tables in book form, but there are a number of factors that you need to consider.

First, and this may seem obvious, *never* write about a color work that you know only in black-and-white reproduction. Not only are you likely to make a mistake about the nature or feel of the work, but you are unable to discuss what may be one of the most important features of the work, its use of color. In Courbet's *Burial at Ornans*, for instance, a distinct positive/negative effect is created in the play of black and white between

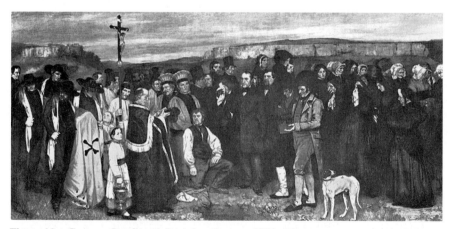

Figure 10   Gustave Courbet, *A Burial at Ornans*, 1849. Oil on canvas,
10 ft. 4 in. × 21 ft. 11 in. Musée d'Orsay, Paris. Giraudon/Art Resource, New York.

the two sides of the painting, a play accentuated by the dominance of red on the left side of the canvas, especially in the dress of the comical beadles. All this is lost in reproduction and, as a result, the unifying structure—and tension—of the painting's color scheme is lost as well.

Second, pay very close attention to the dimensions of the work, given in the caption to the reproduction (often this detail will be found only in a "List of Reproductions," or similar section, in a separate part of the book). Imagine, as accurately as possible, the size of the piece with which are dealing. Is it very small, or very large? Does your sense of its size alter your response to it? It matters greatly, for instance, that you understand that the figures in Courbet's *Burial at Ornans* are nearly life-size, that the painting is over 10 feet high and nearly 22 feet long.

Third, recognize that even in the best reproductions you can get only the vaguest sense of a particular work's texture, the tactile qualities of its surface, its literal "feel." In Cubist collage, for instance, it is often impossible to tell, except in the actual presence of the work, whether a particular passage in the work is drawn, painted, or glued on. A piece of delicately grained wood might be brown paper with the grain drawn on in pencil, or it might be simulated wood-grained wallpaper pasted onto the canvas, or it might be an actual piece of wood. Such distinctions might be important in a discussion of the Cubist artist's delight in undermining traditional notions about distinctions between the artificial and the "real."

Finally, the quality of color reproduction varies widely, from book to book and even from image to image within a book. It is a good idea, whenever possible and especially when color is an issue that seems important to your discussion, to consult as many reproductions as you can locate. If there seems to be some question as to which reproduction is most accurate, ask your professor for an opinion. Very often your professor will have seen the work firsthand. You can also turn to the Internet. Most museum Web sites tend to display works in their collection on their Web sites in very true color. This cannot be said of other non-museum Web sites, however, where color quality varies as greatly as it does in print.

THE COMPUTER AND "THE MUSEUM WITHOUT WALLS"

If, in the last century, photo reproduction in books created a "museum without walls," the development of the computer and the introduction of the Internet has tumbled the museum's walls even more dramatically. In one of the earliest essays surveying the possibilities of art research on the

Web, "The Internet as a Research Medium for Art Historians," Leif Harmsen of the Art History Research Centre (**html://www.harmsen.net/ahrc**) reminds us of both the possibilities offered by Internet research and its limitations:

> The world wide web is a method of serving texts, images and other digital objects that are kept on many computers across the internet. It represents a sea of inconsistent and unverified information from all corners of the world. While each web object has its own discreet *universal resource locator* (URL), this is where any uniform web-wide standard for organisation ends. There is no standard cataloguing system over the global network as there often is within particular institutions or a unified database structure. Consequently, the web is neither a graceful nor complete index of any kind . . . but it is another possible means to find relevant information that might not be at a local library or mentioned in any traditional index. For the good researcher the web is like the proverbial stone that must not be left unturned.[11]

These words are as accurate today as they were when Harmsen wrote them in 1996. The Web is an extraordinarily awkward instrument of sometimes astonishing power and potential.

The great museum collections of the world are becoming increasingly accessible online, to the great benefit of art students everywhere. The collection of the National Gallery in Washington, DC, for instance, is available on the World Wide Web at **http://www.nga.gov**. The Web site not only contains good reproductions of the museum's collection, including details of individual works, but also short essays about many of the works. An aspect of the site particularly valuable to K–12 teachers preparing art curricula is NGAKids, which contains detailed interactive explanations of many of the museum's more famous works and related activities suitable for the classroom.

Many of the works in the massive collection of New York's Metropolitan Museum of Art are viewable on the museum's Web site, **http://www.metmuseum.org**. On arriving at the site, choose "Curatorial Departments" from the "What's Online" bar. This will take you to a menu displaying the museum's various departments—"Arms and Armor," "Egyptian Art," "Medieval Art," "European Paintings," and so on. Here, each department features fifty or more highlights from their collections. If you are searching for works by a particular artist—say, Cézanne—type his name in the "Search" feature. This will take you to a "Search Options" page, where you can choose to browse the Museum's online collection for Cézanne, an option that results in thirty-four works of art, most of them in color and all of which—including, for instance, Figure 25 in this book, Cézanne's *Mont Sainte-Victoire*—can be enlarged for closer study. Of these, twenty-three are actually the work of Cézanne. The eleven others are works that are related in some manner to him—for instance, Courbet's

Woman with a Parrot, a small photograph of which, the Web site tells us, Cézanne carried in his wallet. Some of the Met's online reproductions include a "Zoom" feature—in the case of Cézanne, his *Still Life with Apples and a Pot of Primroses*, from the early 1890s—which allows you to examine details of the work of art at very close range. Even greater detail is available in the ImageBase of the Fine Arts Museum of San Francisco, **http://www.famsf.org**, where the site's zoom display options enable the visitor to see blown-up details of the more than 85,000 works of art in its collections. As a result, the student can see, online, details of work that heretofore could only be viewed in person.

One of the most useful art sites on the Web can be found at **http://www.artcyclopedia.com**. There you can search by artist's name, by title of the work, or by museum. Searching by artist's name will provide you with a comprehensive and regularly updated list of museum and other sites where reproductions of a given artist's work are available for viewing. Another excellent site for works from the medieval era into the nineteenth century is The Web Gallery of Art, **http://www.wga.hu**. A Web site like the online Picasso Project, **http://www.tamu.edu/mocl/picasso**, created by Dr. Enrique Mallen at Texas A&M University, provides a month-by-month illustrated biography of Picasso, extensive bibliography and archive sources, as well as reproductions of over 13,000 artworks.

Information about individual artists and their works is accessible by most of the standard Web search engines—two of the best are Yahoo!, at **http://www.yahoo.com**, and Google, at **http://www.google.com**, both of which have image search capability. By typing in an artist's name and, often, the title of a work, you can usually find reproductions in the "Images" section of these two sites. But be very careful. Color quality can vary dramatically. For instance, if you were to search for the painting that arguably gave Impressionism its name, Monet's famous *Impression Sunrise* (by typing in Monet Impression Sunrise), the results would yield dozens of images of markedly different coloring. How do you know which is most accurate? Poster sites are notoriously unreliable. But even the Marmottan Museum site, in Paris, where the painting is housed (**http://www.marmottan.com**), yields a vastly over-exposed reproduction. A reasonably accurate reproduction can be found at a site that is almost always reliable, Mark Harden's Artchive (**http://www.artchive.com**), which contains some 2,000 quality downloadable scans.

One of the best places to begin a search for architecture is at a site maintained by Jeffrey Howe of Boston College, Architecture Links on the World Wide Web, **http://www.bc.edu/bc_org/avp/cas/fnart/archweb_frames.html**. Another useful site is The Great Buildings Collection at **http://www.greatbuildings.com**, which features not only reproductions of the world's greatest buildings but commentary by their architects and other useful links. A search of the Great Buildings site can be combined with a search of one of the leading architectural magazines, *Architecture Week*, at **http://www.architectureweek.com/search**. This is a particularly useful place to begin if you are researching the work of twentieth-century and contemporary architects.

Increasingly, artists are creating their own Web sites. For instance, David Reed, whose inclusion of his own painting into a still from Alfred Hitchcock's *Vertigo* so fascinated Arthur Danto (see the Introduction), maintains a site at **http://www.davidreedstudio.com**. The site contains not only numerous reproductions of his paintings and installation projects, but, under "Information" in the sidebar, interviews with the artist, his writings (including an essay explaining his intentions in creating the Hitchcock-inspired installations, entitled "Scottie's Place / Judy's Place," and critical essays on his work by both European and American scholars.

Some museums even allow you to download their images and use them to illustrate your paper, provided the museum is properly cited (more on this in later chapters) and that your use is entirely educational, not-for-profit, and that you do not distribute the project (e.g., don't put it on the Web and don't present it outside of class). The **artcyclopedia.com** Web site conveniently notes which museums and image archives allow personal and educational use of their images, including, incidentally, Mark Harden's Artchive. If the museum does not specifically grant such permission on their site, you *must* ask for permission before downloading and reproducing any image. Be careful about simply using an image found on another Web site. Many Web sites are constructed with images that are reproduced without permission and infringe on copyright. The fact that someone else has used an image (with or without permission) does not mean that you may also. It is also important to recognize that even if a work of art is hundreds of years old—and so, it would seem, in the public domain—the reproduction on the Web is not the work of art itself and is therefore subject to contemporary copyright as a photograph in its own right.

SUMMARY

You should approach the selection of a work to write about from a book with more or less the same degree of awareness and caution that you would employ in selecting a work to write about in a museum or gallery. In sum:

1. Determine in what ways the space of the museum or gallery (or the book) is potentially influencing your expectations. Have you come to the Guggenheim, for instance, because you want to see modern art?

2. Examine the context of the work of art that initially attracts you and determine in what ways that context informs your understanding of the work. Imagine it in some other context. Does this alter your perception of it? Are you attracted to the work despite its context or, and this is much more often the case, because of its context? Are you considering the work *as art* because you are seeing it in a museum or gallery?

3. Have you chosen a work that is rich enough to sustain an interesting essay? Will you have enough to say?

4. Have you chosen a work that interests you? Does it seem to pose special problems? Are you surprised at your interest in it? Can you begin to articulate what is interesting about it?

5. Are there other works that interest you as well? Do they seem to have something in common with the work that initially caught your eye? Do they shed light on it? Would discussing one or more of them help you to explain what interests you in the first work? How are they different? How are they the same? What kinds of continuity can you establish between them? What kinds of change are apparent?

6. Even if you find nothing of real interest to you, can you imagine that someone of relatively sophisticated taste and developed intelligence must find these works interesting enough to justify their exhibition, and can you begin to determine what the source of that interest might be?

These are all questions that you need to ask yourself even before you begin to write. They will help put you in the proper spirit—that is, in a *questioning* frame of mind. Even more to the point, they are likely to help you understand your own feelings about the work or works you want to write about before you begin to write your essay.

USING VISUAL INFORMATION

What to Look For and How to Describe What You See

Probably the greatest stumbling block for most people confronting the prospect of writing about art for the first time is what they take to be the specialized vocabulary of the art connoisseur, a vocabulary with which they are not conversant. Actually, the vocabulary of good art writing is relatively simple and based on common sense. What is more esoteric and sometimes totally alien to the uninitiated is the jargon of technical and period styles that has developed as a sort of shorthand descriptive tool—a rhetoric that includes words like "classical," "baroque," "romantic," "modern," and "postmodern." If these words were not useful, they would not have the wide circulation that they do, but it is not necessary to feel comfortable with them in order to begin writing about art. They originate out of distinctions among the ways that subject matter, the more common elements of form, certain principles of composition, and questions of media are employed. Most of you are quite familiar with the less specialized vocabulary of art writing—words like "line," "color," "balance," "rhythm," "sculpture," and "video"—and this more usual (and useful) vocabulary is far less threatening and more accessible than concepts such as "baroque." But there are many ways in which you can use this less specialized vocabulary to your benefit as a writer. What does it matter, for instance, that an artist employs line in a certain way, or that the elements in a painting repeat themselves in a visual rhythm?

It is important to point out here, again, that all art worth the name is a question of conscious choices. Given two points and the opportunity to draw a line between them, you can choose to draw a straight line, or a curved line, or a line that turns back on itself and meanders hither and yon until it finally ends. Your choice, which may or may not be deliberate and studied, reveals a good deal about your temperament and even about the way you approach the world in general. A work of art is a compendium of such choices. Artists, who make such choices as a matter of habit and profession, make them a good deal more deliberately than you and I. This is not to say that artists necessarily think out in advance the implications of every line they make, or every application of color. Any artist will tell you that much of what they do is intuitive. However, every artist has the opportunity to revise and redo each work, each gesture—and indeed, very often artists take advantage of that opportunity. It is probably safe to assume that what you are seeing in a work of art is an *intentional* effect, that the artist knows what he or she is doing.

A summary of the kinds of choices an artist can make follows. Any work of art involves the artist in choosing among a number of different possibilities: the *subject matter* must be decided upon; the artist must choose which of the various available *media* is best to portray or express that subject matter; in achieving the work, the artist will employ the *formal elements*, such as line and color, in the distinctive and particular ways that are part and parcel of the artist's style or that express the artist's intentions in a clear way; and, finally, the artist will decide how best to organize these elements into a whole by means of what we call the *principles of design* or *composition*. The following sections will give you some sense of the things you need to consider when you are trying to decide what a particular work of art might be about or why it might be significant or interesting. This is by no means a complete survey of the various media, principles of design, or formal elements that artists have at their disposal. It is simply an outline of why an awareness of them might help you learn to ask the right types of questions and then write a better essay. If you need more information about any given element or principle, you can consult any of the many authoritative art appreciation texts, where most of this material is treated in greater detail.

CONSIDERING THE SUBJECT MATTER OF THE WORK

Subject matter is the sum of the identifiable objects, incidents, and iconographic or narrative references that are recognizable in a work of art. In representational painting, these references are sometimes clear, but even in representational painting, they can be obscure. **Iconography** presents a special problem. Iconographic references are symbolic conventions that are widely recognizable in a given culture: for instance, the meaning of the cross or a crown of thorns is widely known in the Christian West. But recognition of iconographic references depends upon one's familiarity with the culture at hand. A Buddhist might not understand such references at all, just as most Christians probably would not understand the iconographic significance of the different positions of Buddha's hands in sculptures representing him. Even within a given cultural tradition, the iconographic significance of various elements in works of art can be lost over time or even change. Thus, the iconographic significance of various elements in many medieval paintings is fiercely debated by scholars, for example, a dog at the feet of a lady in a Renaissance painting might represent fidelity but in a later, Baroque painting by, say, Rubens, the presence of a dog might represent our basest animal instincts.

Very often simply consulting the title will make a work's range of reference more explicit. In abstract painting, however, the title may or may not help you understand the subject matter of the work. *Full Fathom Five*, the title of the Jackson Pollock painting discussed in the next chapter (Figure 31), is very helpful indeed, but *Untitled*, the "title" of many of his later works, is far less so—except, of course, insofar as it asks us to question why he chose not to title his later works. It is possible to say of Pollock's untitled paintings that since they announce no overt reference, their subject matter might be paint—or the act of painting itself.

One of the most important things for you to remember when discussing subject matter is that it is in no way comparable to the *meaning* of the work. One of the classic examples of this distinction between subject matter and meaning was developed by Joshua C. Taylor in his handbook, *Learning to Look*. Taylor points out that Pietro Perugino's *Crucifixion with Saints* (Figure 11) and Carlo Crivelli's *The Crucifixion* (Figure 12) have the same subject matter, but the meaning that subject matter assumes in each is dramatically different. For Taylor, the Perugino "would seem to quell the possible anguish and effects of suffering which might be associated with the scene and to establish a serenity and calm, a complete relaxation of the emotional and physical forces which might be expected to operate in connection with such a subject matter." In contrast, in the Crivelli there "is no rest, no calm, or contemplation. Instead we take upon

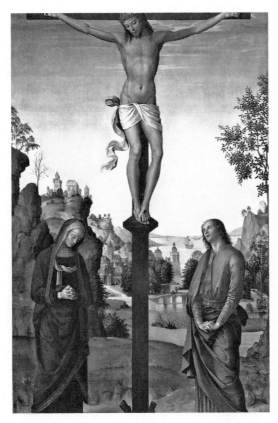

Figure 11   Pietro Perugino, *The Crucifixion with the Virgin, Saint John, Saint Jerome, and Saint Mary Magdalene* (central panel), c. 1485. Oil on panel transferred from wood to canvas, 39⅞ in. × 22¼ in. National Gallery of Art, Washington, D.C. Andrew W. Mellon Collection.

ourselves the anguish and physical hurt which seem to motivate the actions of the figures. And nowhere is there escape, no point on which our attention can fix itself to bring order to our excited emotions."[1] There are many structural and formal reasons for this difference—and Taylor's analysis occupies ten pages of text—but it should be sufficiently clear that whatever meaning these works possess, it is independent of subject matter. It is as if one artist sees in the scene the promise of salvation hereafter, whereas the other sees the misery of our life on earth in the here and now.

One of the most common mistakes student writers make is to confuse subject matter with meaning. A typical sentence describing one of these paintings might read: "Perugino [or Crivelli, take your pick] has painted a crucifixion, with all that implies." The assumption here is that the meaning of the crucifixion is clear, but such assumptions often stymie the

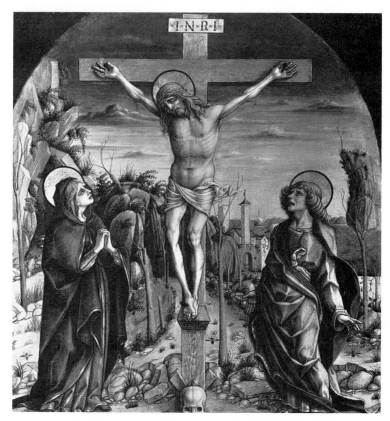

Figure 12   Carlo Crivelli, *The Crucifixion*, c. 1480–1490. Tempera on panel, 29½ in. × 21¾ in. Wirt D. Walker Fund, 1929.862. The Art Institute of Chicago. Photograph © The Art Institute of Chicago. All rights reserved.

development of ideas. The crucifixion may imply something very specific to the student writer, but Taylor's point is that the crucifixion implies something entirely different to each painter, and that implication may or may not coincide with what the writer feels about the same subject matter.

One way to assess the meaning of a given work, then, is to try to imagine other handlings of the same material. It should follow that one of the best ways to write an essay about Perugino's *Crucifixion* is to *compare* it with Crivelli's. From the differences between the two we are able to recognize some of the important decisions that Perugino made and thereby learn a great deal about his intentions.

Or imagine a painting of a red barn in a green field. What does it matter that it is bathed in sunlight? What is the effect of the startling color contrast between red and green, and how would the same scene feel handled monochromatically as a winter scene, in the snow, at dusk? Does it matter that the barn is silhouetted against the summer sky and that your point of view is relatively low? Does it make a difference that its lines and angles are clearly delineated? Would it seem less appealing, more lonely and foreboding, if it melded into the landscape and shadows? In short, given just such a set of questions and a broad enough selection of barn paintings, a reasonably significant essay on American attitudes toward landscape could probably be written. Similarly, art historians will often illustrate the difference between two stylistic periods or schools by comparing works of similar subject matter but distinctive handling. Even particular phases within an individual artist's career can be understood by means of this device. What, for instance, are the obvious differences in handling between the two versions of *Mont Sainte-Victoire* by Paul Cézanne that appear later in this chapter (Figures 24 and 25), the second of which was painted nearly twenty years after the first? Don't you suppose that this difference tells you something about Cézanne's intentions?

Thus, while subject matter (or the lack of it, in a nonobjective painting) is the most readily apparent aspect of the work, it is also, by itself, one of the least useful in discussing the work's meaning. Rather than asking yourself what the subject matter of a particular work is, ask yourself, "What does the artist think of his or her subject matter?"

What artists think of their subject matter will be revealed in their handling of the various formal elements, the way they employ the principles of composition, and their choice of medium.

DESCRIBING THE FORMAL ELEMENTS YOU DISCOVER IN THE WORK

Line

A line is any relatively narrow, elongated mark. It is the primary means we have for defining visual form, and it stands to reason that it is one of the most important elements to be considered in preparing to write about a work of art. The difference in its use in the Perugino and Crivelli *Crucifixions* probably accounts, more than anything else, for the difference in meaning that we detect in these works. In the Perugino, line is determined largely in relation to the strong vertical and horizontal axes defined by the cross itself. Working off these axes are a series of isosceles triangles, the most obvious of which is defined by the relative positions of the heads of the Virgin Mary and St. John at the two bottom corners, and Christ's head at the apex. The apex and central axis of each of the composition's other triangles remain constant, but a wider, higher triangle can be seen stretching across Christ's feet, each side defined by the trees left and right; another is defined by the outside legs of Mary and St. John, their toes pointing to the bottom corners of the triangle, and another by the almost perfectly balanced sweep of their garments across their legs. A smaller, more precise set of triangles can be seen emanating from the diamond shape of the cross at Christ's feet. Most subtle of all, this pattern is repeated in the folded fingers of both the Virgin and St. John. The curvilinear features of this painting, from the disposition of St. John's arms to the arched bridge in the background, seem to wrap around this triangular structure in the same manner that a circle fits neatly around an equilateral triangle.

In contrast, and although the cross divides the canvas more or less along the same geometric axes as in the Perugino, not a single line in the Crivelli seems to work in harmony with any other. If line seems to function in a more or less centripetal way in the Perugino, it is centrifugal in the Crivelli, as if erupting from the scene. Most tellingly, the painting's lines all seem to fall away from the central axis. Both the Virgin's and St. John's head tilt back rather than in toward the path of their gaze. St. John's hand points away from the scene. The effect is not unlike the curious sense of disorganization achieved by Courbet in his *Burial at Ornans* (Figure 10). Despite the strong horizontal order achieved in Courbet's grouping, especially in relation to the landscape behind, and the verticality of the figures (a horizontal and vertical structure emphasized, as it often is in Western art, by the crucifix rising over the scene), Courbet fragments the composition by having each gaze—including the dog's—turn in a different direction. There is no *focus* to the scene. Implied lines of sight explode in every direction away from the supposed center of attention, the burial itself. Similarly, in the Crivelli the nervous fractures of the cliff at the painting's bottom serve to create a general sense of linear disorder that stands in stark contrast to the linear regularity and harmony of the cross, let alone the balance of the Perugino. This disorder is emphasized especially by the curved crack that seems to emanate from the skull, together with the clutter of linear detail in the painting—tufts of grass here and there, tree limbs reaching every which way.

To emphasize this difference, Taylor contrasts the treatment of St. John in both paintings. In the Crivelli, he notes,

> the vertical structure-line of the figure [i.e., the fact that he is standing up in a more or less vertical way] has little meaning with regard to the effect of the whole, because the diagonal lines of his cloak are so strong that they destroy all possible sense of a vertical compact mass. And consider the nature of the lines themselves. Every curve is flattened and broken so that the line seems to struggle to reach its destination. Furthermore, if we isolate the line of the

cloak, we see that far from suggesting the balanced arc of a circle, it seems rather like the lash of a whip. And this eccentric line is repeated throughout, in the robe of the Virgin, in the rocks, and even in the body of Christ. How contrasting with this is our scheme of the St. John of Perugino. The lines of the Perugino seem to wrap themselves together into a smooth-planed volume, while those of the Crivelli disperse into the air.[2]

Even more than in the figure of St. John, the difference between the two paintings is manifest in the way that each recessional plane in the Perugino is clearly outlined, the landscape receding into the distance in a reasonable and logical way, while in the Crivelli the landscape seems hopelessly confused. Notice, in the Crivelli, how the drapery on Christ's right leg sweeps in a continuous line into the landscape beyond, how the tree, which must be some distance behind him, seems to catch the drapery in the wind, and how another tree behind St. John seems to merge into the cliff across the bay. In contrast, each plane in the Perugino is distinct. Line seems to serve a regulatory function. It is as if line preserves the integrity of the space it describes in the Perugino, whereas in the Crivelli it violates that integrity, disrupting our sense of organization, order, and harmony.

Shape and Space

It should be obvious, from the previous discussion, that one of the primary functions of line is to describe shape and space. One of the first questions to ask yourself about a work of art is *how* do its lines describe shape and space? In a consistent and orderly way? Or in an apparently disruptive, even random way?

Normally, shape and space are defined in consistent and accessible ways, although the lines operating to define these elements may not always be immediately obvious to you and may achieve very complicated effects. But if you learn to see these lines in the first place, and the shapes or spaces they describe, you can begin to come to grips with other, more complicated effects achieved by the artist. When you first look at Claude Monet's *Gare Saint-Lazare, Paris* (Figure 13), for instance, you may not notice the diamond-shaped space that defines the center of the composition. Its top is defined by the roof of the train station, and its bottom is delineated by two implicit or compositional lines that meet in the hazy locomotive in the center distance and that run along the tops of the two closer locomotives on each side of the center track. The area is very interesting because it seems to describe both shape—a two-dimensional diamond on a flat plane—and space—the airy volume of the train station itself. In fact, the bottom two lines are achieved by Monet's reference to the traditional laws of *mechanical perspective*, the geometric system of compositional lines perfected in the Renaissance for rendering the illusion

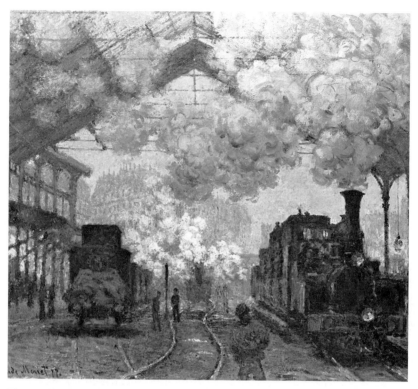

Figure 13   Claude Monet, *Gare Saint-Lazare, Paris: The Arrival of a Train,* 1877. Oil on canvas, 32¾ in. × 40 in. Courtesy of The Harvard University Art Museums. Bequest, Collection of Maurice Wertheim, Class of 1906. 1951.53.

of three-dimensional space. Often imaged as a road (or set of railroad tracks!) disappearing into the distance, traditional perspective is based on the observation that parallel lines seem to converge toward a common point in the distance, referred to as the *vanishing point*. In the Monet, the tops (and bottoms) of the trains converge on a hypothetical vanishing point that exists directly across from our point of view, somewhere behind the distant central locomotive. The serpentine central railroad tracks would also converge on this point if they were straightened out.

Thus, the bottom of the diamond shape is composed of two lines that define three-dimensional space, while its top is composed of the two lines that define the two-dimensional edge of the roof. Monet seems to be willfully playing off the illusion of three-dimensional space against the actuality of the two-dimensional surface of the canvas (paintings are, after all, two-dimensional planes), a sense of play that the curvilinear railroad tracks emphasize since they seem to be themselves a joke on the traditional representation of the laws of perspective. Why would Monet want to do this? Would it surprise you to discover that he was interested in drawing our attention not only to his choice of subject matter, but to his handling of it as well? Doesn't it make sense that he might want you to consider the surface of the canvas as a composition of effects to be enjoyed in their own right? His style of painting was as new in 1877 as the steam locomotive itself, and we move between them, the subject and its handling, in much the way that our eye moves between the two-dimensional design of the surface and the three-dimensional representation of space.

While Monet does not quite say that the design of the composition is more important than its subject matter, it is quite clear that, along with a number of his contemporaries, he initiates a logic that will eventually argue just that. Franz Kline's's *Mahoning* (Figure 14), painted in 1956, almost eighty years after the Monet, has made that very step. Here the canvas is all surface; there is no illusion of depth; there is only a criss-crossed tangle of broadly painted lines. This is a very difficult type of painting for most students to talk about because it seems to have no

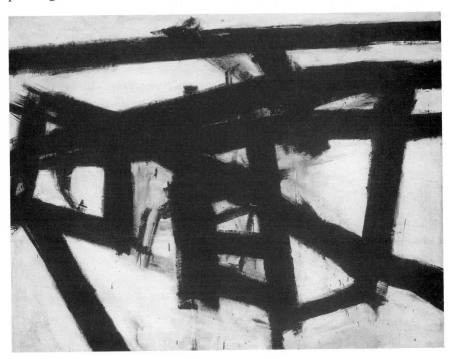

Figure 14   Franz Kline, *Mahoning*, 1956. Oil on canvas, 6 ft. 8 in. × 8 ft. 4 in. Whitney Museum of American Art, New York. Purchased with funds from the Friends of the Whitney Museum of American Art. Photo: Steven Sloman. Collection of the Whitney Museum of American Art, New York.

subject matter. If you consider, however, that one of its primary objectives might be to free the painted surface of the necessity of representing three-dimensional space, then you might discover that you have something to say after all. Like Jackson Pollock's *Full Fathom Five*, discussed in the next chapter (Figure 31), the painting is about *painting* itself, the act of painting.

In the late 1940s, Kline had projected a number of his representational drawings onto a wall. So magnified, they seemed to him to capture a sense of dynamic tension that mirrored the force and energy of the modern world. Mahoning is, in fact, the name of a township in Carbon County, Ohio, very near to where Kline grew up in Lehighton, an industrial city in the heart of Pennsylvania's coal country. As a child, Kline was surrounded by factories, foundries, and, especially, the trestles and rails of the Lehigh Valley Railroad, which carried anthracite coal down the valley and was the city's largest employer. *Mahoning* does not represent the industrial landscape of Kline's youth, but it does *suggest* it. In the broad strokes of his brush on canvas, one senses the furious activity of industrial America.

Light and Dark

Kline did not think of his painting as black lines on a white ground. "I paint the white as well as the black," he said, "and the white is just as important."[3] The tension between black and white—that is, between opposites, light and dark—is one of the primary sources of the sense of energy that Kline's canvases evoke. But Kline also understands that in addition to the traditional systems of geometric perspective, one of the primary ways to evoke the illusion of three dimensions on a two-dimensional plane in painting is by imitating the effects of light as it falls on three-dimensional surfaces. His painting, in effect, violates that expectation, and as a result, turns its back on the representation of three-dimensional space.

Gradual shifts from light to dark across the same surface generally indicate that you are looking at a rounded or contoured form. Georgia O'Keeffe's charcoal drawing of *Alligator Pears in a Basket* (Figure 15) is an almost classic example of this modulation, ranging from the darkest blacks in its shadowed areas, through shadings of gray, to areas of white where an intense light strikes directly off the foremost surface of the pears or off the back of the basket itself. This technique of creating the sense of a rounded surface by means of gradual shifts and gradations of light and dark was perfected in Renaissance Italy, where it came to be known as *chiaroscuro*. In Italian, *chiaroscuro* means light (*chiaro*) dark (*oscuro*)—and

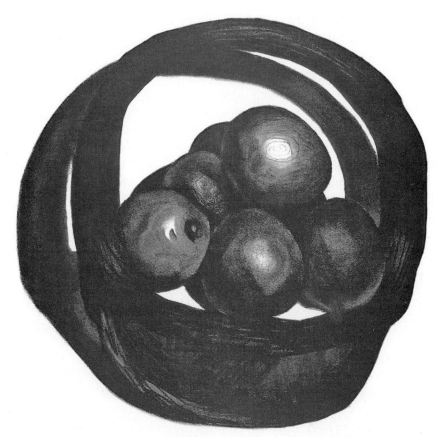

Figure 15　Georgia O'Keeffe, *Alligator Pears in a Basket*, 1923. Charcoal on paper, 24⅞ in. × 18⅞ in. The National Museum of Women in the Arts, Washington, D.C., Gift of Wallace and Wilhelmina Holladay. © 2005 The Georgia O'Keeffe Foundation/Artist Rights Society (ARS), New York.

notice how language here reflects technique, as the end of the first word melds into the beginning of the second, creating a seamless transition between "light" and "dark."

The relative level of lightness or darkness of an area or object is traditionally called its relative **value**. That is, a given area or object can be said to be darker or lighter in value. In O'Keeffe's *Alligator Pears*, the areas of the pears closest to the source of light are lighter in value than those farther away. These areas, which directly reflect the light source and which are indicated by white, are known as *highlights*. Highlights are often left "blank," revealing the unmarked paper or canvas beneath. As the object moves through the shadings of gray to dark black, different depths of shadow are evoked. Darker even than any shading on the object itself is its *cast shadow*, seen here at the bottom left. Note that just above the cast shadow, at the bottom of the basket, is an area of light gray. This is an area of reflected light, cast indirectly from the table on which the basket rests, lightening the underside of the shadowed surface.

The revelation of form and space through chiaroscuro and shifts in value is one of the primary techniques of printmaking, used to great effect in Käthe Kollwitz's etching *The Downtrodden* (Figure 16). Perhaps more than any other printmaker in history, with the possible exception of Rembrandt and Goya, Kollwitz was able to manipulate contrasts of light and dark to create highly dramatic and emotional images. In this etching, the figures barely emerge from a shroud of darkness. Only the edge of the father's hand, which hides his face in the upper right corner of the composition, and the angelic face of the dead child in the lower left corner are fully lit. Between these poles of light, poles of innocence and despair, the

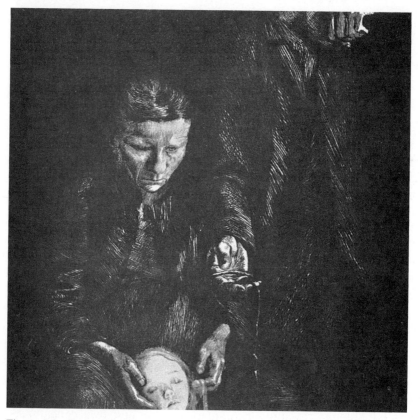

Figure 16   Käthe Kollwitz, *The Downtrodden*, 1900. Etching and aquatint on paper, 12⅛ in. × 9¾ in. The National Museum of Women in the Arts, Washington, D.C. Gift of Wallace and Wilhelmina Holladay. © 2005 Artists Rights Society (ARS), New York/VG Bild-Kunst, Bonn.

mother reaches down, letting the child's hair fall between her fingers. Just above, the father's hand reaches out aimlessly. And the mother's face, realized in a powerful middle-tone gray, displays an extraordinary range of emotion, at once infinitely sad and ultimately tired. It is as if Kollwitz's gray has become the very color of bitterness and resignation.

Sometimes you will encounter works of art that employ little or no contrast between light and dark. The light seems uniform throughout. If the drama in Kollwitz's etching is palpable, minimal contrasts of light and dark usually have the opposite effect. A work of art that seems uniform in tone, such as Perugino's *Crucifixion*, usually evokes feelings of calm and harmony.

Color

Though it is easier to think of questions of light in terms of black and white, the same rules apply to color as well. Think, for instance, of the difference between pink and maroon: one is red saturated with white and the other is red saturated with black. When we refer to someone who wears a lot of pastels, we mean someone who dresses in colors light in value. It is not hard to imagine a painting of a red ball that moves in value from a white highlight to a black shadow through all the various tints and shades of red (the color that results from adding white to a pure hue is called a *tint* of that hue, and the color that results from adding black to the hue is called a *shade*).

Yet color functions in works of art in terms more complicated than just those of light and dark. In fact, in the same way that black and white can be considered opposites, each color has its opposite number as well. These opposites are called *complementary* colors. Complements are pairs of colors that, when mixed together in almost equal proportion, create neutral grays, but that, when standing side by side, as pure hues, seem to intensify and even contradict one another.

The traditional color wheel (see the back cover) makes these oppositions clear. Each primary color—red, yellow, and blue—has, as its complement, a secondary color—green, violet, and orange, respectively. Thus, the standard complementary pairs are red/green, yellow/violet, and blue/orange (and, obviously, the intermediate hues have complementary opposites as well—the complement of red-orange is blue-green, for instance). Furthermore, just as gray moderates between black and white—as white becomes gray with the addition of black and vice versa—each color gradually moderates into the hue of its neighbor with the addition of its neighbor. Thus, the more yellow one adds to green, for instance, the more yellow-green the color becomes. Neighboring colors on the color wheel are called *analogous* colors. Unlike complementary pairs, which create a sense of contradiction or opposition to one another, analogous pairs usually seem to rest harmoniously beside each other. The analogous blue-green-violet relationships are commonly referred to as *cool*, and red-orange-yellow combinations are said to be *warm*, or even hot.

Color theory is a vastly complicated field—one that is hardly settled, even among physicists—and the scheme described above is a vast over-simplification of the ways in which colors interact. (If you wish to explore color interactions more fully, try to locate Josef Albers's *Interaction of Color*, originally written in 1963, but reissued in 1993 in an interactive CD-ROM edition by the Yale University Press. Here you can have hands-on experience manipulating and experiencing the properties of color in a simple, easily accessible format.) Nevertheless, in writing about art, it is important to understand the basic complementary and analogous group-ings because a great many works depend upon them to some degree in order to achieve their effects.

Much of the power of Vincent van Gogh's work depends upon his use of complementary color schemes. In a letter to his brother Theo, he described his famous painting *The Night Café* (Figure 17) in the follow-ing terms:

> In my picture of the "Night Café" I have tried to express the idea that the café is a place where one can ruin oneself, run mad, or commit a crime. I have tried to express the terrible passions of humanity by means of red and green. The room is blood-red and dark yellow, with a green billiard table in the middle; there are four lemon-yellow lamps with a glow of orange and green. Everywhere there is a clash and contrast of the most alien reds and greens in the figures of little sleeping hooligans in the empty dreary room, in violet and blue. . . . The white coat of the patron, on vigil in a corner, turns lemon-yellow, or pale luminous green.
> So I have tried to express, as it were, the powers of darkness in a low wine-shop, and all this in an atmosphere like a devil's furnace of pale sulphur. . . . It is color not locally true from the point of view of the stereoscopic realist, but color to suggest the emotion of an ardent temperament.[4]

The color scheme, especially the contrast between the complements red and green, is meant to suggest the tension of the scene, the sense that beneath the surface an almost violent energy or fury is about to erupt. Things do not go together here, either literally or pictorially.

In a painting such as Pablo Picasso's *Woman with Book* (reproduced on the back cover), virtually the full range of complementary contrasts is employed. Yet, perhaps surprisingly, the painting seems to be unified in its overall effect. Except for the presence of a profile that does not seem to be her own in the mirror behind the seated woman—an image that suggests

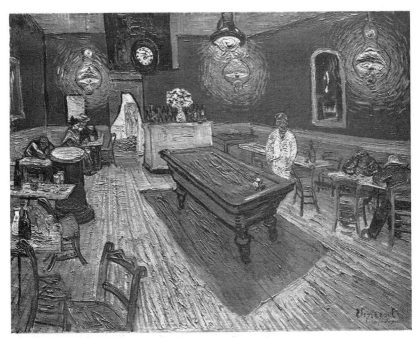

Figure 17   Vincent van Gogh, *The Night Café*, 1888. Oil on canvas,
28½ in. × 36 ¼ in. Yale University Art Gallery, Bequest of Stephen Carlton Clark,
B.A. 1903. 1961.18.34. Photograph by Jospeh Szaszfai.

an intruder or an unseen observer, perhaps the painter himself—nothing
of the tension and turmoil of van Gogh's painting seems to inform our vision. Rather, we observe a woman in meditation, gazing vacantly up from
her book, daydreaming. Picasso's painting, as opposed to van Gogh's, is
not a nightmare, but a reverie.

     This is surely the result, in part, of Picasso's subject matter: His
model is Marie-Thérèse Walter, who was also his mistress. But it is also a
result of the fact that he is trying to make contrasting elements work together in harmony. Just as he has rendered the face of Marie-Thérèse simultaneously in both profile and three-quarters view, just as he made her
seem at once fully clothed and half-naked, Picasso's sometimes stridently
discordant colors here manage to coexist. It is apparent from the blackness
outside the window to the left that it is night, and the darkness outside
contrasts strongly to the brightness inside. Notice how the shadowed side
of Marie-Thérèse's face is rendered in green and violet and how these two
colors dominate the darker, cooler side of the painting. On the other side
of the painting, the warm red glow of the chair, its orange back topped by
the yellow frame around the mirror, seems almost to generate heat. It is as

if Picasso has realized here something of which van Gogh only dreamed. In the same letter to his brother Theo in which he described the color effects of *The Night Café*, he claimed that he was always in hope of expressing "the love of two lovers by a marriage of two complementary colors, their mingling and their opposition, the mysterious vibrations of kindred tones."[5]

Neither Picasso nor van Gogh is interested in representing the precise color of the scene. The Impressionists had freed painting of the necessity of representing *local* color (that is, the color we "know" a thing to be in the sense that we "know" trees are green) and chose to represent the *optical* color of what they saw (in the sense that a hill covered with "green" trees will appear to be blue in the distance). Picasso and van Gogh have gone even further. "Colors, like features," Picasso would later write, "follow the changes of the emotions."[6] As opposed to van Gogh's, however, Picasso's emotions here run toward the loving and affectionate. One of the most widely known books of Picasso's day was an occult classic, first published in 1901, called *Thought-Forms*, written by Annie Besant and C. W. Leadbeater. It contains a "Key to the Meaning of Colors" outlining which emotions are connected to which colors, and not surprisingly, mint green, the color of Marie-Thérèse's hair, is the color of "sympathy," and violet, the other color that dominates her face, suggests "love for humanity." More precisely, violet is "a mixture of affection and devotion . . . and the more delicate shades of [it] invariably show the capacity of absorbing and responding to a high and beautiful ideal."[7] Picasso might not have read the book, but its classifications were so popular that he almost could not have escaped them, and, evidently, they are at work here.

It should be clear, however, even from this brief discussion, that different artists use color in different ways. Yellow may be "sulphurous," as it was to van Gogh, but to someone else it may suggest the "highest intellect"—the meaning, in fact, given it by Besant and Leadbeater. Combinations of complementary colors may create tension in a painting, or they may be harmonized. Analogous color schemes often create a unified effect, but just as often that sense of unity can transform itself into a feeling of monotony. Meaningful discussions of an artist's use of color must often rely on a context greater than the individual work—as I have relied on the artist's own words, in the case of van Gogh, and upon intellectual history, in the case of Picasso.

As a writer, you must always be aware of the fact that the associations you have with a particular color are not universal. If you hear "red," you may think "roses" and "love," while the next person thinks "blood" and "anger," while the next person thinks "communism." If van Gogh's lines seem violent and disruptive, for instance, this impression would support your notion that he is employing complementary colors in order to create a sense of disunity and chaos. Ask yourself, how does the artist employ color and what does it mean? *But then ask yourself*, do other things about the composition support this reading?

Other Elements

There are a number of other formal elements that might be important for you to consider. What, for instance, is the *texture* of the work? If it is uniformly smooth, does this smoothness contribute to a sense of harmony? Consider van Gogh's *Night Café* again. Doesn't the thickness of the brushstroke, its very assertive and gestural presence, express his emotional involvement in the scene at the café?

Another formal element, one not quickly associated with art, is time. Time becomes a factor in sculpture when we find ourselves walking around or through it. Sculpture changes as the light changes, in the play of light and shadow across the surfaces of the work. This must have been the effect of the great free-standing sculptures that once adorned the pediment of the Parthenon in Athens. One of the surviving fragments of the east pediment, which originally depicted the birth of Athena, is the so-called *Three Goddesses* (Figure 18). Slightly larger than lifesize, the sculpture stood on a three-foot-deep platform over fifty feet above the ground. As the sun moved from directly in front of it to its apex at noon,

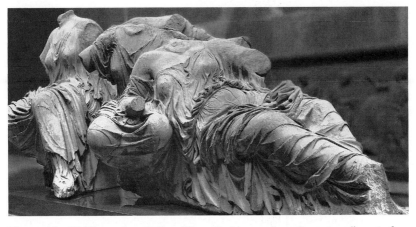

Figure 18   Phidias and workshop, *Three Goddesses*, from the east pediment of the Parthenon, c. 435 B.C. Marble, height of center figure 5 ft. The British Museum, London.

the detailed folds of the draperies, falling across the highly defined bodies of the goddesses, would have made the sculptures almost seem to move and come to life. The sculptor—or at least the sculptor overseeing the work, since he was in charge of the entire sculptural program at the Parthenon—was the famous Phidias (c. 490–430 B.C.). He was reknowned for his ability to recreate the human form in a convincing way. Sculpture, to him, was a dynamic, rather than static, medium. It was active rather than passive. It seemed to be alive.

Even abstract contemporary sculpture can achieve something of the same effect. The garden Isamu Noguchi designed for the museum dedicated to his work in Long Island City, Queens, is a dynamic space (Figure 19). In Japanese gardens, each of the stone sculptures is believed to be connected to the others, as if each were rising out of the great mass of the earth's core. We enter a garden, we recognize that we are "floating" on the world beneath. As we move through it, the garden changes. As Noguchi himself describes it: "Its viewing is polydirectional. Its awareness is in depth. With participation of mobile man all points are centered. Without a fixed point of perspective all views are equal, continuous motion with continuous change."[8] Noguchi also feels that the stones in a garden

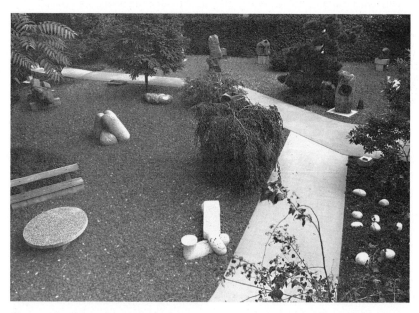

Figure 19   Isamu Noguchi, Sculpture Garden, Isamu Noguchi Garden Museum, Long Island City, Queens, New York, 1987. Published with the permission of The Isamu Noguchi Foundation, Inc. © 2005. The Isamu Noguchi Foundation and Garden Museum, New York/Artists Rights Society (ARS), New York. Photo by Shigeo Anzai.

embody a sense of time comparable to human time: "Their weathering seems to coincide . . . with our own sense of historical time. . . . There is a time passage to stone not unlike our own. A mellowing takes place."[9] Thus in the garden we experience time in its vast geological sense (through the stones' connection to the earth mass below), in terms of the span of human life, and in "real" time, as we walk through the garden in the present moment itself.

Time entered the domain of art in radically new terms with the invention of photography in the nineteenth century. Photography seems to convey the essence of a particular time and place, and this aura of authenticity, together with its sense of instantaneous vision, of the moment itself captured forever, constitutes a large part of its appeal. Today, it is apparent that the dialogue between the present moment of our seeing the photograph—our actual experience of it in "real" time—versus the way in which the photograph seems to embody, or make present, something long lost or far away, has revolutionized our sense of time and space.

But it is important to recognize that the photograph is composed of the same elements as the other arts. The photographer Henri-Cartier Bresson described the photographic process in the following terms:

> We must place ourselves and our camera in the right relationship with the subject, and it is in fitting the latter into the frame of the viewfinder that the problems of composition begin. This recognition, in real life, of a rhythm of surfaces, lines, and values is for me the essence of photography. . . . We compose almost at the moment of releasing the shutter. . . . Later you can amuse yourself by tracing out on the photo the geometrical pattern, or spatial relationships, realizing that, by releasing the shutter at that precise instant, you had instinctively selected an exact geometrical harmony, and that without this the photograph would have been lifeless.[10]

Cartier-Bresson called this the "decisive moment." Thus, the leaping man in his 1932 photograph *Gare St. Lazare* (Figure 20) is suspended above his own reflection, which creates a sense of balance in the photograph. But his leap is also reflected on the circus poster on the wall behind him, just as the semicircular arched back of the poster figure is echoed in the semicircular form in the foreground water. In fact, the reflection in the water eerily mirrors the poster on the wall.

Two other art media—video and film—rely even more on time. One of the traditional distinctions among the arts has been that the plastic arts—painting, drawing, and sculpture—are *spatial* media, while the other arts—dance, music, literature—are primarily *temporal* and *linear* in nature. Video and film are both.

Most of us think of video in relation to commercial television. However, many video artists purposefully manipulate the medium in order to

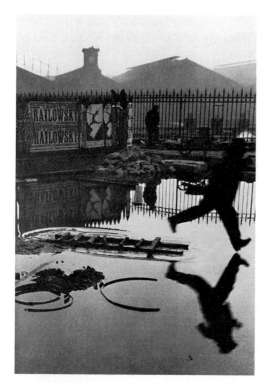

Figure 20   Henri Cartier-Bresson,
Gare St. Lazare, Paris, 1932.
Magnum Photos Inc. © 2002
Henri Cartier-Bresson.

distinguish what they do from the television we habitually consume. The most common difference, again, is the medium's relation to time. Standard television time is based upon the length of the commercial—10, 30, 60, and, less commonly, 120 seconds in duration. As David Antin has pointed out in a detailed analysis of the medium, there is really no difference between commercial time and the structure of time in television programs generally. A news "story," for instance, generally fits into this same time scheme, and a baseball game is a succession of pitches, hits, and catches that fit the same pace.[11] Video artists often ignore this pace completely, so to a viewer expecting "television," their work usually seems boring. Very commonly, the camera is held in one position, for as long as an hour. In this way, other aspects of the medium that are generally ignored, such as the peculiar way that video represents and distorts deep space, are foregrounded.

Video artists also commonly create installations in which the viewer encounters the medium as part of a larger, sculptural space. Bill Viola's *Room for St. John of the Cross* (Figure 21), for instance, contrasts the stillness of a single image of a mountain shown on a small monitor in a cubicle at the center of the room (a space comparable to the "meditative"

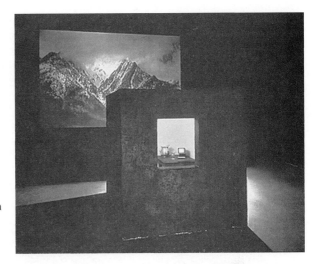

Figure 21 Bill Viola, *Room for St. John of the Cross*, 1983. Video and sound installation. © Bill Viola. Collection: Museum of Contemporary Art, Los Angeles. Photo by Kira Perov/Sauidds and Nunns.

space of St. John) and a video projection of large snow-covered mountains, shot with a hand-held camera in wild, breathless flights of movement. The world "outside," in other words, contrasts with the world "within."

Perhaps one of the best ways to think of film, which can reproduce space in ways far more sophisticated than can video, is as an assemblage of various spatial and temporal points of view. The fade-in and fade-out, flashback and flashforward, closeup and longshot, and even the multi-image screen, all combine to produce film's many, sometimes startling visual effects. This multiplicity of visual techniques combines with the more purely temporal means of narrative, dialogue, and musical score to create one of the most complex of the arts.

Photography, film, and video have come to play an important role in contemporary art as means to document live, temporary, or remote works. As much as Richard Serra would prefer for us to have experienced *Tilted Arc* in person, we know it today primarily through its photodocumentation. The artist Christo and his wife, Jeanne-Claude, purposefully create large-scale works that are in place for, at most, a few weeks. On June 24, 1995, for instance, the Christos completed wrapping the Reichstag in Berlin (Figure 22). Originally completed in 1894 to house the German parliament, the building has great significance to the German people. Soon after Hitler had become chancellor in 1933, it had been burned, an act symbolic of Hitler's desire to end parliamentary rule. Destroyed again in 1945 during the Battle of Berlin, it was rebuilt during the Cold War as a symbol of West Germany's dedication to democracy, but it was unclear what function it should actually serve. With the reunification of Germany

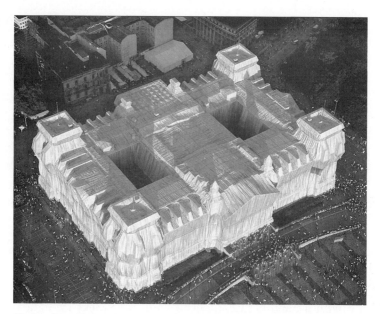

Figure 22   Christo and Jeanne-Claude, *Wrapped Reichstag*, Berlin, 1971–95. © Christo 1995. Photo by Wolfgang Volz.

in 1990, the lower house of the German parliament, the Bundestag, moved in, an act symbolic of renewed German unity. The Christos had wanted to wrap the Reichstag since 1971, but were continually denied. Finally, in 1994, the Bundestag voted 292 to 223, with 9 abstentions, to let the Christos proceed. The wrapping required 1,076,000 square feet of woven polypropylene fabric with an aluminum surface and 51,181 feet of blue rope. Thousands of people, both in person and on the Internet, watched as 90 climbers and 110 workers created a wall of folds and draperies reminiscent of Greek sculpture (see Figure 18). When the building was unwrapped two weeks later, on July 7, it became clear that the Christos had succeeded in giving the people of Germany a "gift," a celebratory renewal of the Reichstag.

The Christos' works are always short-lived, "living on" only in the memory of those who saw them and in the array of drawings, models, photographs, and films that survive the actual work. As a result, many of their works—*Running Fence*, an 18-foot-high, 24 ½-mile-long, white fabric fence that ran through two northern California counties in 1976; *Surrounded Islands*, in which eleven islands in Biscayne Bay, Florida, were wrapped with pink fabric in 1983; and the 1991 *Umbrellas, Japan— U. S. A.*, in which 1,760 almost 20-foot-tall yellow umbrellas were opened in the Tejon Pass in southern California at the same time that 1,340 blue umbrellas were opened in Ibaraki prefecture, north of Tokyo, Japan— have achieved an almost mythological status. The creation of this mythology is a fundamental part of the Christos' work. Their monumental endeavors acquire something of the aura of the ruined monuments of ancient civilizations.

Finally, of all the new media, the computer and digital technologies associated with it have offered the artist a unique new set of possibilities, opening the image to the possibility of manipulation by both artist and audience. Photography, once thought of as a medium of evidentiary "truth," a record of the visual world, has become, in the digital age, a medium in which new visual worlds can be created. Take, for instance, the work of German photographer Andreas Gursky. Many of his large photographs are completely unmanipulated, "straight" renderings of the contemporary world, but many others, such as the enormous *Untitled V* (Figure 23), may well capture the "truth" of contemporary experience but are themselves complete fabrications. To create *Untitled V*, Gursky built a short double shelf, which he then photographed six times, restocking it with new shoes in each instance—there are 204 sets of Nike running shoes in the work— and then repositioning his camera to create the proper angle. Finally, he pieced each of the six shots together to make the final image, a sort of testimony to commodity culture, NikeTown gone monumental. If this panorama of commerce is technically "inauthentic," it seems, nevertheless, an "authentic" icon of contemporary life.

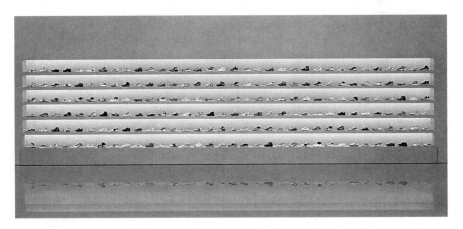

Figure 23   Andreas Gursky, *Untitled V*, 1997. C-Print, 73 in. × 174¼ in. Courtesy of the Mathew Marks Gallery, New York. © 2005 Andreas Gursky/Artists Rights Society (ARS), New York/VG Bild-Kunst, Bonn.

RECOGNIZING THE PRINCIPLES OF DESIGN

One thing that would suggest that the traditional distinction between spatial and temporal media might not be altogether valid is the sense of visual rhythm and repetition we often experience before works of art. Certain formal elements—lines, shapes, colors—recur, in either exact or analogous terms, and this repetition creates a sense of visual rhythm that is analogous to musical or poetic rhythm. In all the arts, rhythm and repetition serve to organize, or order, the work into distinct and recognizable patterns.

Rhythm and Repetition

Paul Cézanne's *Mont Sainte-Victoire* (Figure 24) is composed of a number of repeated shapes and lines that serve to unify the composition. Notice that the slope of the mountain itself is repeated down the right edge of the top of the central tree, again with uncanny accuracy in the branch that extends from the right side of the tree halfway down its trunk, and

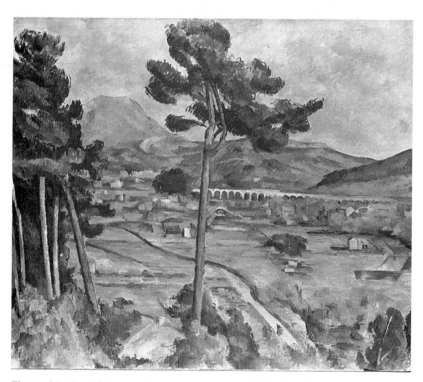

Figure 24   Paul Cézanne, *Mont Sainte-Victoire*, 1885–87. Oil on canvas, 25¼ in. × 32⅛ in. The Metropolitan Museum of Art, Bequest of Mrs. H.O. Havemeyer, 1929. The H. O. Havemeyer Collection (29.100.64).

again, immediately below that, in the large curve of the river. The shape of the river on the left of the tree seems to echo, in reverse, the hill that comes into the composition from the right. A rhythm of arches extends the length of the railroad viaduct, and throughout the painting, small, square, and rectangular areas—buildings, roofs, chimneys, fields—echo and re- peat each other's shapes. In a later version of this same motif (Figure 25), the precise elements of the landscape have virtually disappeared, yet here the small quadrilateral shapes—which now seem to have been created by single brushstrokes, moving in a sort of pulse through the composition— ascend toward the top of the mountain in a rhythm and movement of growing clarity and definition finally achieved by Cézanne at the paint- ing's (and the mountain's) summit.

Balance

If you compare Cézanne's 1885–1887 version of *Mont Sainte-Victoire* (Figure 24) to Perugino's *Crucifixion* (Figure 11), you will notice that one thing these very different paintings have in common is that they can be

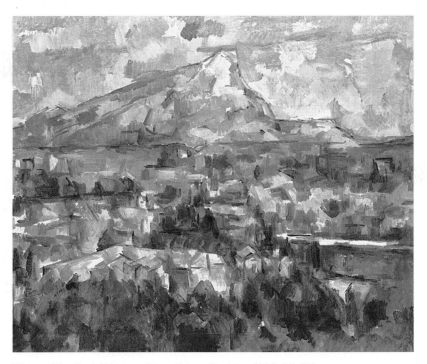

Figure 25   Paul Cézanne, *Mont Sainte-Victoire*, 1904–06. Oil on canvas, 27⅞ in. × 36⅛ in. Philadelphia Museum of Art, George W. Elkins Collection. E1936–1–1.

divided into more or less equal quarters across the axes formed, in the Cézanne, by the central vertical tree and the arched railroad viaduct and, in the Perugino, along the vertical axis of the cross and the horizon line. This geometric division, which echoes and reinforces the shape of the frame in each painting, creates a sense of symmetry and equilibrium in both compositions. The sense of disequilibrium apparent in Crivelli's *Crucifixion* (Figure 12) derives in large part from the fact that, despite its overall symmetry and balance on a vertical axis, created by both the cross and the overriding arch, there is no clear horizontal symmetry, and the structure of the right side of the composition seems radically different from the structure of the left. It is as if Crivelli has purposefully defied our expectation of balance.

There are many other ways to achieve a sense of balance in a composition. *Radial balance* is created when all the elements of the composition seem to emerge from a real or actual focal point. Many works of art utilize an *asymmetrical balance* in which a perceived center of gravity seems to balance elements around it. It is like balancing a teeter-totter with a very heavy child on one side and a light child on the other: the heavy child moves toward the center of the teeter-totter, while the lighter child sits on the very end. Furthermore, relatively dark shapes seem "heavier" to the eye than lighter ones.

Sometimes artists purposefully choose to violate the principle of balance. Franz Kline's *Mahoning* (Figure 14) is a case in point. He once commented on the way that black and white exert tension upon one another in his paintings: "I thought about it in a certain sense of the awkwardness of 'not-balance,' the tentative reality of lack of balance."[12] His contemporary, the abstract painter Milton Resnick, described the feeling in similar terms. In his painting, he said, "I'm falling. I keep from falling. I'm falling. I keep from falling."[13] For both, the lack of balance helped to create a sense of action and energy in the painting.

Proportion

Proportion is the relationship of each part of the composition to the whole and to each other part. An excellent example of its use can be seen in the 1904–1906 version of *Mont Sainte-Victoire* (Figure 25). You will notice that the composition is divided neatly at the foot of the mountain. This line, with the mountain and clouds above it and the countryside of Aix-en-Provence in southern France below it, very closely corresponds to what the ancient Greeks referred to as "the golden section." This proportion—which is found, incidentally, in living organisms—can be defined mathematically as follows: The smaller section (in the Cézanne, the area above the line running across the bottom of the mountain) is to the larger section (the countryside below) as the larger section is to the whole painting. In numbers, each ratio is 1 to 1.618. Not only did the Greeks use this "ideal" or "perfect" proportion as the basis for constructing their greatest buildings, but they conceived of the human body in the same terms. The perfect body, they reasoned, consists of a torso and head roughly equivalent to the vertical height of the top of the Cézanne composition, the body from the waist down equivalent to the lower part of the composition. Such proportional ideals, it is worth suggesting, dominate our visual thinking to this day—from our sense of when a landscape painting "feels" right to our sense of the ideal human form.

Scale

Scale is an issue with which we have dealt already in relation to the "museum without walls." It is sometimes very difficult, for instance, to get an accurate feeling for a work of art's size from a photograph of it. To get a sense of this principle, you need only think again of the actual size of Courbet's *Burial at Ornans* (Figure 10) and the viewer's inability to take it all in at once, compared with the sense of containment one feels before it in reproduction. Similarly, only from a series of photographs or from the film can you get a sense of the many elements of Noguchi's Sculpture Garden (Figure 19). Part of the extraordinarily comic effect of Roy Lichtenstein's monumental sculpture *Brushstroke* (Figure 35) derives from the fact that it is so large, not only in relation to a normal brushstroke but in relation to the Hirshhorn Museum, which rises behind it.

Other, more subtle effects can be achieved by manipulating scale. In Cézanne's 1885–1887 *Mont Sainte-Victoire* (Figure 24), for instance, there appears to be a large bush or tree at the end of the railroad viaduct just to the left of the central tree. If it were really a tree, however, it would be 300 or 400 feet tall. It is, in fact, part of the pine in the foreground. In a very subtle move here, Cézanne purposefully draws the most distant planes of the canvas up to the closest by confusing our reading of what is near and what is far away. As a result, our attention is drawn to the surface of the composition, to its organization as a design, as much as to its representation of a three-dimensional world.

Scale is relative. That is, we define the scale of an object in terms of its relation to other objects around it. Thus, the two video images in Bill Viola's *Room for St. John of the Cross* (Figure 21) are very different in scale—one large, one small—and this difference in scale contributes to the work's disorienting sense of space. In another example, the artist Nikolai Buglaj has transformed a classical example of an optical illusion created by a shift in the context in which objects are perceived into a

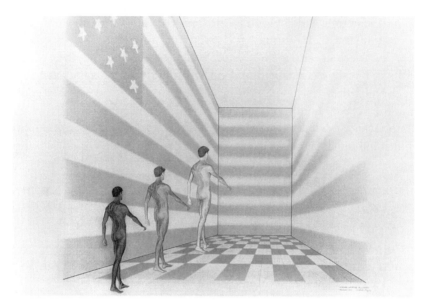

Figure 26   Nikolai Buglaj, *Racial Optical Illusion*, 1997. Pencil and ink on paper, 30 × 40 in. Courtesy the artist.

commentary on race relations in the United States (Figure 26). The three figures in this piece are all the same size (if you don't believe it, measure them for yourself), but because the figure outside the room is, in effect, contextless, he looks small. The figure entering the room appears to be larger, and the figure inside the room appears largest of all. The surrounding walls alter the relative scale in which each figure is perceived. The wall of the room is decorated with an American flag, and it represents, for Buglaj, the "system" from which African Americans are excluded, thus making them appear smaller than they are. Conversely, from the outside looking in, the white man appears larger than he really is.

Unity and Variety

One of the primary sources of interest and power in many works of art is the way their various elements are combined to create a sense of oneness or unity. Picasso's *Woman with Book*, for instance, on the back cover, is almost wildly diverse in its color, but its pattern of repetitive shapes unifies it. Round forms—from necklace, to armchair, to Marie-Thérèse's breasts—draw the various colors together, as do the teardrop shapes that make up both sleeves of Marie-Thérèse's dress as well as the bodice of her dress. In fact, the pattern of interlaced curves that circulate around and across the model's body unifies the entire composition.

CONSIDERING QUESTIONS OF MEDIUM

Each of the different media—painting, printmaking, drawing, sculpture, architecture, photography, video, film, fiber, ceramics, metal, and glass, among others—has its distinctive qualities, and within each there are various subcategories—in painting, for instance, there is oil, acrylic, watercolor, tempera, gouache, and so on—that can elicit far different effects in themselves. One of the most important differences between the Perugino and Crivelli *Crucifixions* (Figures 11 and 12), which we have so far not discussed, lies in the artists' choice of medium. The first is an oil painting, while the second is painted in tempera. As we have already noted, oil paint is translucent—light penetrates it and is reflected back—and thus Perugino's medium contributes to the painting's sense of hopefulness, its seeming promise of salvation. Tempera, on the other hand, is opaque, and, unless varnished, its flat, matte finish seems dull compared to the glowing surface of an oil painting, qualities perfectly in keeping with the prevailing sense of misery in Crivelli's work.

Sometimes a given medium is particularly suitable for conveying a given set of ideas. Black-and-white film, for instance, lends itself particularly effectively to the portrayal of tension and opposition. Shirin Neshat, an Iranian artist who came to the United States in 1979 to study art, was struck, eleven years later, when she finally returned to her homeland, by the profound change that had occurred. Color had disappeared and everything was black and white—the men dressed in white shirts, the women in traditional black *chadors*, head-to-toe coverings that reveal only face and hands. The *chador*, especially from the Western perspective that Neshat brought with her upon her return to Iran, represents the oppression of women in Islamic society, but within the context of Islam, many women believe that they are truly equal to men, and they claim that the *chador*, by concealing a woman's sexuality, prevents her from becoming a sexual object. This tension is the subject of Neshat's 1999 video installation *Rapture* (Figures 27a and b). Composed of two videos projected simultaneously on opposite walls, on one side of the room a group of men are seen in a fortified castle, where they engage in ritual activities. On the other side, women approach the castle, observe the men, then turn their back on the males' activities, walk to the sea, where six of them climb into a boat setting themselves adrift. On the opposite wall, the men, who have gathered on the ramparts, wave goodbye, as if the gulf that separates men from women in Islamic culture is, at least partially, unbridgeable.

Video, in other words, brings the tensions implicit in the still image to life. As a medium, it animates the photograph. Something of the same

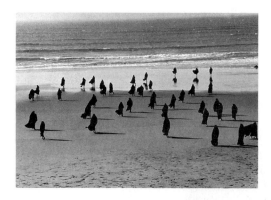

Figure 27a and b   Shirin Neshat, *Rapture*, 1997. Two video production stills. © Sherin Neshat 1999. Courtesy Barbara Gladstone Gallery, New York.

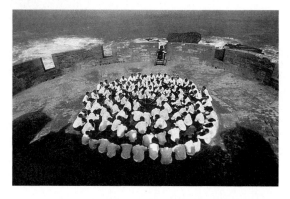

effect is achieved in the relation between, say, the drawings of a Michelangelo for the ceiling of the Sistine Chapel at the Vatican in Rome and the finished fresco, or between Christo's preparatory collage drawings for his projects such as *The Gates* (Figures 28 and 29) and the fully realized piece, which was installed in New York's Central Park in the winter of 2005. Although the collages represent one of the principal ways that Christo and Jeanne-Claude raise the funds necessary to create their work—they accept neither private nor foundation support—they also document the evolution of Christo and Jeanne-Claude's ideas. They are, additionally, as Christo has said, "works of art on their own," even if the experience of the actual installation is a vastly different experience. To see a piece like the *Wrapped Reichstag* (Figure 22) or *The Gates* in person is, in Christo's words, "a little bit like if you are a sportsman, if you climb the Himalaya. In a way it is the unrepeatable experience. It cannot be substituted with anything, not the film, or the photographs, nor books, nor records can substitute that art experience."[14]

BEGINNING YOUR ESSAY BY DESCRIBING THE WORK

One of the best ways to begin an essay on a work of art is to describe it as accurately as possible. Description serves two purposes. On the one hand, it orients your readers by drawing their attention to what you believe are the most salient features of the work. But perhaps more important,

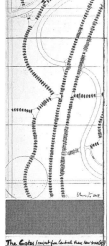
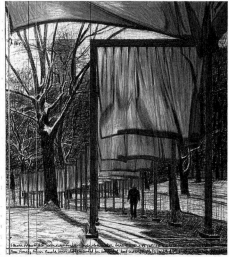

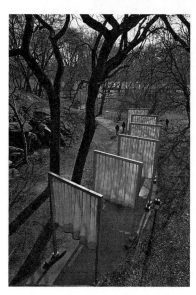

Figure 28 (above)   Christo and Jeanne-Claude, *The Gates*, Project for Central Park, New York City, 2004. Collage: Pencil, fabric, charcoal, pastel, wax crayon, enamel paint, map and fabric sample; in two parts: 30½ in. × 12 in. and 30½ in. × 26¼ in. Photo by Wolfgang Volz, © Christo 2004.

Figure 29 (right)   Christo and Jeanne-Claude, *The Gates*, Project for Central Park, New York City, 1979–2005. Photo by Wolfgang Volz, © Christo 2005.

description forces you to scrutinize the work yourself. In the process of describing the work well, considering not just its subject matter and medium but its formal elements and principles of composition, you will almost always gain a better understanding of the artist's intentions and more fully grasp the meaning of the work.

The following description of a photograph by Walker Evans (Figure 30) was written by a student, Richard Watson, as part of a final exam essay in a course on the history of photography. Before reading on,

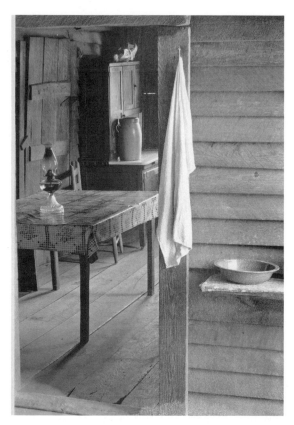

Figure 30   Walker Evans, *Washroom and Dining Area of Floyd Burroughs's Home, Hale County, Alabama,* 1936. 35mm photograph. Courtesy of the Library of Congress, Washington, D.C.

you might find it useful to jot down a few of your own notes describing the photograph so that you can compare your own descriptive abilities to Richard's. Remember, I think Richard's description is exemplary, and if your description does not quite measure up to his, that is probably as it should be. Richard's descriptive abilities were nowhere nearly this developed when he first began writing about art, some three years and seven art history classes before he wrote the essay from which this description is excerpted.

> Evans's creation is a symphony of shapes,
> textures, lines, and planes. The round washbasin
> sitting on the rectangular shelf, in front of al-
> ternating thick and thin horizontal wallboards, the
> vertical doorframe, the square kitchen table with

its multifaceted curved and shaped kerosene lamp, the beefy square kitchen hutch with its rectangular upper cupboard, and the elegant pitcher with its graceful curves, all contribute to the geometric harmony of this quiet setting. The textures of the rough wooden doorframe, the back door set against the smooth floorboard, the soft tablecloth, and the polished glass lamp and pitcher offer an array of tactile sensation. Most notable is the towel hanging in the center of the photograph, which together with the heavy vertical doorframe cuts the composition in half and provides the focal point of the composition.

By combining simple geometric shapes, Evans has created a powerfully dramatic composition. The elements of light and darkness (enhanced by his choice of medium, black-and-white photography) generate a tension of opposition and harmony among the shapes and produce a unique sense of balance: the white towel against the dark doorframe, the black table leg and its shadow cutting across the brightly sun-lit floor, and the sun-drenched pitcher framed by the black back wall, all generate a play of light and dark. The effect is enhanced by the thick bands of grayish wood in the front wall, chopped into equal parts by the thin black lines of shadow that separate them. The vertical frame of the door, the table legs, and the upper part of the kitchen hutch rise in juxtaposition to the horizontal plane of the front wall, the door's header, creating a series of short, rigidly uniform lines. The diagonal run of the wide floorboards, broken by thin, dark joints is echoed by the broad kitchen table, the lined tablecloth, and the sun-bathed work space of the kitchen hutch.

This description formed the basis of Richard's essay. Although he went on to place the photograph in a larger context—it was one of many Evans created for the Farm Security Administration during the Great Depression and it was reproduced without commentary in the opening pages of *Let Us Now Praise Famous Men,* a work he published with writer James Agee in 1941—Richard argued that the formal eloquence of the photograph mirrored Evans's and Agee's overall purpose. Both writer and photographer wanted to reveal the inherent dignity of Alabama's impoverished sharecroppers. The order and harmony of the scene elevate the banal and humble to the level of art.

ASKING YOURSELF ABOUT THE WORK OF ART: A SUMMARY

The following set of questions derives from the previous discussion and is meant as a quick reminder of the kinds of things you might ask yourself about a work of art. It is by no means complete, and you almost surely will discover that most works of art raise still other questions. Nor will every question be of particular importance in your coming to terms with each work you see. Still, this summary list does provide you with a model of the kind of analytical process that will help you understand what you see. (These questions are reproduced inside the front cover so that you can readily access them.)

One last word of warning: Don't take these questions as an outline of your eventual paper. Good essays are never written by answering a series of predetermined questions. Consider them, rather, as a guide designed to help you take the notes and organize the thoughts that will eventually lead to writing a good essay.

QUESTIONS TO ASK BEFORE WRITING ABOUT A WORK OF ART

What is the subject matter of the work?

- What is its title?
- Does the title help you interpret what you see?
- Can you imagine different treatments of the same subject matter that would change the way you read the work?

What formal elements are important to the work and how do they relate to its subject matter?

- How is line employed in the work?
- Does it seem to regulate or order the composition?
- Does it seem to fragment the work?
- Is it consistent with traditional laws of perspective or does it violate them?
- What is the relation of shape to space in the work?
- How do light and dark function in the work? Is there a great deal of tonal contrast, or is it held to a minimum?
- What is the predominant color scheme of the work? Are complementary or analogous colors employed?
- What other elements seem important? Is your attention drawn to the work's texture? Does time seem an important factor in your experience of the work?

How are these elements organized?

- Is there significant use of visual rhythm and repetition of elements?
- Is the composition balanced? Symmetrically? Asymmetrically?
- Do the work's various elements seem proportional, and how does the question of scale affect your perception?
- Does the composition seem unified or not?

How has the artist's choice of medium played a role in the presentation of the various elements and their organization or design?

- Are effects achieved that are realizable only in this particular medium?
- If more than one medium is involved, what is their relation?

What does all this *mean*?

- What are the artist's intentions? How do these intentions manifest themselves in the composition? Are there other feelings or attitudes that the composition seems to evoke, and what specific elements or design choices account for those feelings?

RESPONDING TO THE VERBAL FRAME

Where Else to Look For Help in Understanding What You See

Every work of art is framed, not just in the way that a painting is contained within either a simple or ornate frame, neither in the way that the "white cube" of the exhibition space "frames" our vision, but by a verbal frame— the discourse that surrounds the work. Artists could be said to write about their works each time they title them. Sometimes they have even more to say. They might contribute an artist's statement to exhibitions or grant interviews about their work. Often they become friendly with professional writers, who in turn write about the work from a more or less "insider" point of view. In time, articles appear and books are published. Vast quantities of material might surround a given artist's work. The more you can take advantage of this verbal frame, the better off you will be. The task of moving from image to word is never an easy one, and by paying attention to the ways in which works of art are described, analyzed, and discussed by others, you can ease your task as a writer considerably.

TAKING THE TITLE AND LABEL INTO ACCOUNT

In the collection of the Museum of Modern Art in New York City, there is a comparatively small, dark green painting by Jackson Pollock (Figure 31). It is, at first glance, not nearly as engaging as some of the larger works by

Pollock or his abstract expressionist colleagues in the museum's collection. It lacks their size and, given the more or less ominous and dense tone of the composition, their visual variety and interest. It is not usually hung in any way that indicates that you should pay special attention to it. You assume, rather, that it is placed here as a kind of antecedent to the later, greater works to follow.

However, it is a very interesting painting, which you might discover if you are lucky enough to find it hanging in the museum and if you have the time and inclination to stroll up to it and read its title: *Full Fathom Five*. This title immediately tells something very specific to someone familiar with Shakespeare's works. But even to someone for whom the phrase is unfamiliar, a certain resonance immediately develops that alters one's sense of the painting. You might know only that the word "fathom"

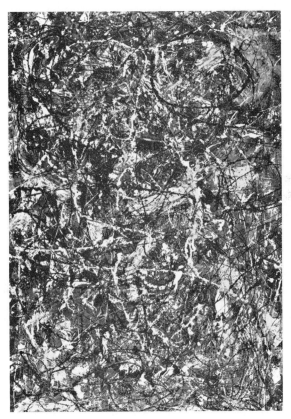

Figure 31   Jackson Pollock, *Full Fathom Five*, 1947. Oil on canvas, with nails, tacks, buttons, key, coins, cigarettes, matches, etc., 50⅞ in. × 30⅛ in. The Museum of Modern Art/Licensed by Scala-Art Resource, New York. Gift of Peggy Guggenheim. © 2005 Pollock-Krasner Foundation/Artists Rights Society (ARS), New York.

is a nautical measure of depth, but suddenly, when you look back at the canvas, at its deep green recesses, you are under water.

The title is the first verbal clue that you are given about the meaning of the work. It never ceases to astonish me how often students simply ignore the title in their discussion of a work of art. A colleague of mine once had a student who began an essay on Marcel Duchamp's *Nude Descending a Staircase* by writing, "In this painting, Duchamp depicts a person going up the stairs." This is a particularly vivid example of a quite common occurrence. The title, in fact, is one of the first pieces of information you must take into account. (Remember, though: very few titles have come down to us from antiquity. The small, prehistoric sculpture commonly known as the *Venus of Willendorf*, for instance, was so named by scholars shortly after its discovery in 1908. "Venus," of course, was the Roman goddess of love, a figure unknown to prehistoric cultures, and the title attaches modern meaning to a figure that may well have nothing whatever to do with love.) Sometimes a title is of no apparent help at all, but even in that case you can surely recognize that, for whatever reasons (reasons that you need to begin to figure out, incidentally), the artist has chosen not to help you, or has decided to confuse you. Not long after Pollock painted *Full Fathom Five*, he stopped naming his paintings and started numbering them. In a 1950 interview with Pollock and his wife, Lee Krasner, in *The New Yorker*, Krasner explained: "Numbers are neutral. They make people look at a picture for what it is—pure painting." Pollock then clarified her point: "I decided to stop adding to the confusion. . . . Abstract painting is abstract. It confronts you." [1] You may feel, in the case of *Full Fathom Five*, that the title does indeed add to the confusion. You probably will know that it's a quotation, but you may not recognize that it's from Shakespeare, let alone which play (more than one student has assumed that it's a reference to Jules Verne's *Twenty Thousand Leagues Under the Sea*). Nevertheless, it is worth suggesting that the difference between *Full Fathom Five* and some of the later, large-scale Pollock paintings is that *Full Fathom Five* doesn't engulf you in the way that a painting over eight feet wide might. *Full Fathom Five* is a comparatively small, dark painting. It needs its title.

When you encounter a title you don't understand, ask somebody if they recognize what it refers to. Or consult *Bartlett's Dictionary of Quotations*. The multivolume *Oxford English Dictionary*, although intimidating, can be particularly useful for old-fashioned and archaic meanings, since each entry consists of a history, with examples, of the various usages any given word has undergone. Whenever there's a word in a title that you don't understand, look it up. Sooner or later, the reference will usually become clear.

Pollock's reference, in *Full Fathom Five*, is to Shakespeare's play *The Tempest* (even the title of this play seems to resonate in the dark swirl of the canvas). Early in the play, Ariel, an "airy spirit," as Shakespeare calls him, sings this song to Ferdinand, the son of the King of Naples, who has just come ashore after a shipwreck in which, he believes, his father has been lost. The song leads him to believe that the island is somehow magical and enchanted:

> *Full fathom five thy father lies;*
> *Of his bones are coral made;*
> *Those are pearls that were his eyes;*
> *Nothing of him that doth fade*
> *But doth suffer a sea-change*
> *Into something rich and strange.*
> (*Tempest*, I, ii)

These are words that help you understand the painting. Pollock has led you in their direction, and he intends for you to consider them. They *frame* the painting in a way you cannot afford to ignore.

What they suggest, first of all, is that some sort of "sea-change" has occurred in the painting that has transformed its elements into something "rich and strange." You should ask yourself, "Well, what are the elements of this painting?" Is there anything special about them? Again, if you were to go back to the label accompanying the Pollock painting, to the verbal frame, you would find some additional help. It reads: "Jackson Pollock, *Full Fathom Five*, 1947. Oil on canvas, with nails, tacks, buttons, key, coins, cigarettes, matches, etc., $50\frac{7}{8} \times 30\frac{1}{8}$ in." Looking more closely at the painting, you can see all manner of things buried in the paint, held in place by the sweep and swirl of Pollock's line. Here's a coin, a nail, a screw, a comb, and there's the key—the key to what? you wonder.

Inevitably, the thought arises that these "things" have been transformed—"suffered a sea-change"—by entering into this "painting," a painting that Pollock has implicitly characterized as "rich and strange." Taken together, the elements of the verbal frame, as we have so far established it, can help us begin to understand the exact nature of this transformation. We have moved from the recognizable and the world of the commonplace—nails, coins, and combs—to the virtually unrecognizable and "strange" world of the painting itself—and if this painting seems strange to you now, imagine how it must have appeared in 1947. The agent of this change seems, in fact, to be painting—more precisely, the act of painting—which has worked on the elements lying on its "ground" in a manner analogous to the sea, covering them, burying them beneath the sand, uncovering them again. If the gestural sweep of Pollock's line can be defined at all, then perhaps comparing it to the ebb and eddy, the churn and swirl of sea and tempest, is as close as one can come. Most important, the title announces that the painting is as much a burial as it is a transformation. Whatever riches it may contain, they lay "full fathom five" below. Nothing in Pollock's entire *oeuvre* (that is, the body of his work) better defines the sense of space one feels before his canvases. One peers deep into this work, and it is dark down below. A few things are visible, hinting at more. But Pollock has buried them forever, beneath the swirl of his paint, and they will never be seen again. Pollock gives you a surface, like the surface of the sea, which you know conceals more than it reveals. He provides you with an unfathomable mystery.

CONSIDERING INFORMATIONAL LABELS ACCOMPANYING THE WORK

Although the Pollock painting in the Museum of Modern Art is not accompanied by any more information than I have already given you, it should not be hard to imagine how more information on the label might help you to come to grips with the painting. A simple citation of the appropriate passage in Shakespeare would be helpful to most people. Many museums do provide this sort of informational label as a matter of course.

Most people spend at least as much time reading informational labels in museums as they do looking at the works of art themselves (and this is not the least reason why *Full Fathom Five* is unburdened by a lengthy text—the Museum of Modern Art is one of the busiest museums in the world, and it must keep "traffic" flowing). If there were a label, however, it might read something like this:

> POLLOCK, Jackson. *Full Fathom Five*. 1947. Oil on canvas, with nails, tacks, buttons, key, coins, cigarettes, matches, etc. $50\frac{7}{8} \times 30\frac{1}{8}$ in. Gift of Peggy Guggenheim.

> This painting is one of the first canvases in which Pollock introduced the "all-over" method for which he is famous. By dripping or pouring his paint from sticks or hardened brushes onto canvas tacked to the floor, he was able to liberate his paintings from any sense of being subjected to the inhibiting constraints of traditional, conscious technique. They seemed to spring, now, from unconscious sources. Pollock's title, then, taken from Ariel's song in Act I of Shakespeare's *The Tempest*, suggests a movement below the surface of things and into the unconscious, into a world where painting is transformed, in Ariel's words, into "something rich and strange."

I have limited myself here to approximately 100 words, pretty much the maximum that the public can readily assimilate from a label accompanying an individual work of art. I could say a great deal more—but the very fact that much more can be said is precisely why, as a writer, you can gain not only a great deal of information from labels such as this, but valuable direction for further research and inquiry as well. When you read (and copy) the information on a label, almost inevitably you will recognize what other information might be of value to you.

Given the label above, you would look up the reference to Shakespeare in order to see if there is, in Ariel's song, anything else that might be of use—and there is, as I have already suggested. You would almost certainly want to look at the paintings Pollock executed in 1946 just before this work—some samples of which are in fact close by in the museum—in order to look at how the "inhibiting constraints of traditional, conscious technique" are evident in these earlier paintings. You might want to know about Pollock's interest in the unconscious, and this information, in turn, would probably lead you both to Pollock's own experiences in psychoanalysis and to the influence on Pollock of the French Surrealists, many of whom arrived in New York in the early 1940s in order to escape the war in Europe. The Surrealists emphasized, in their own art, a kind of composition based on "psychic automatism," the dictation of thought in the absence of all control by reason. You might discover, at this point, that many of these French artists circulated around Peggy Guggenheim, who was married to one of them, and that Pollock exhibited almost exclusively at Peggy Guggenheim's gallery—suddenly the brief citation on the label, "Gift of Peggy Guggenheim," takes on a greater resonance.

You might want to read the criticism in order to get a better idea of precisely what that word "all-over" implies. You might even want to follow the history of Pollock's pouring technique as it developed in subsequent years—especially as it relates to the world of images—or his use of concrete things (combs, nails, and so on), which reemerge in his painting after 1950 but which, in *Full Fathom Five*, seem at the brink of completely disappearing beneath the surface of the paint. There seems to be, in other words, an interesting tension, or dialectic, in Pollock's painting between what he calls "pure painting," on the one hand, and reference to the real world, on the other. The relation between the two might be worth exploring. Again, in the Museum of Modern Art there are examples not only of paintings from 1947 to 1950 in which all reference to the world at large seems to have disappeared, but also of later paintings in which recognizable images, even a portrait, reassert themselves.

This is all to suggest that a very substantial essay might easily be developed out of a careful examination of a painting like *Full Fathom Five* and that the conception of this essay would be greatly facilitated by paying attention to the relatively few words that surround the painting as a verbal frame. They are meant to help and inform you. Take advantage of them.

CONSULTING ARTISTS' STATEMENTS AND EXHIBITION CATALOGUES

Very often, especially in one-person exhibitions, an artist's statement, sometimes accompanied by a *curriculum vitae* or brief resume of previous exhibitions and writings about the artist's work, will be available, either in leaflet form or prominently displayed as part of the exhibition. The quality of artists' statements varies widely; one sometimes feels that, asked by a curator or gallery director to provide something of the kind, and feeling, as Pollock did, the work should stand on its own, or that language betrays it, or perhaps out of sheer lack of verbal skill, the artist misrepresents what is going on in the art, intentionally or otherwise. In other words, artists' statements must be approached with caution. However, if they seem to help your analysis of the work, then by all means consider them.

A short statement by Pollock will serve as an example. These comments did not actually accompany an exhibition but were published in a small magazine called *Possibilities* in 1947. Pollock almost certainly considered them to be an "explanation" of what he was up to in his painting, and almost every critic who has come to grips with his art since has relied on them, perhaps because there is so little else to rely on. They have, at any rate, become so central to our understanding of his work that if a one-person retrospective of Pollock's painting were to be mounted today, the statement would almost surely be printed prominently in the exhibition space itself:

> When I am *in* my painting, I'm not aware of what I'm doing. It is only after a sort of "get acquainted" period that I see what I have been about. I have no fears about making changes, destroying the image, etc., because the painting has a life of its own. I try to let it come through. It is only when I lose contact with the painting that the result is a mess. Otherwise, there is pure harmony, an easy give and take, and the painting comes out well.[2]

The famous first sentence—"When I am *in* my painting, I'm not aware of what I'm doing"—refers to Pollock's insistence on his painting's attachment to the unconscious. The most useful phrase here, however, occurs at the end. What Pollock does in this statement is provide you with a vocabulary that you can use to describe his painting—"pure harmony" and "easy give and take." These are things he wants to achieve, and you need to examine the work itself in order to decide for yourself in what ways an "easy give and take" or a "pure harmony" seems to be in evidence. You might argue, for instance, that the tension between the world of things and the world of "pure painting" is embodied in the "give and take" of line as it begins to delineate form or shape and then flies off free. Or you might say that, because Pollock's surface seems to be uniform in intensity, he achieves a sense of "pure harmony." In other words, this vocabulary gives you a way in, something to look for. It helps you to articulate what you see.

The catalogs that sometimes accompany exhibitions can be of even greater help. Even if all the catalog provides you with is reproductions of the works that interest you most, it can be an invaluable aid in writing your essay, a ready reference once you go home. Be sure, however, that the color in the reproductions is accurate: Compare them with the works themselves (don't trust your memory of the color), and if the reproductions are in black and white, note the actual colors separately. Often the catalog will contain essays to help you understand the exhibition in general as well as individual works. When you are writing about works of art that are accompanied by such a catalog, it is best to read the essays *after* your first visit and *after* you have begun to form opinions of your own. Even though the essays are usually written by leading experts, you need not necessarily consider them the absolute last word on the works. The best writing about art—and this is as true of professional writing as it is of student writing—raises as many questions as it answers. You should approach catalog essays in the spirit of initiating a dialogue with them. Let them suggest things to you, let them initiate a line of thought for you to follow that you might not have pursued without their lead, but do not let them have the final word. *Use* the essays, certainly, but to support your *own* thinking.

DISCOVERING OTHER HELPFUL MATERIAL IN THE LIBRARY AND ONLINE

One of the most useful things about exhibition catalogs is that they often contain bibliographies of what has been written about a given artist's work. (The *curriculum vitae* of the artist at a one-person show will often contain a bibliography as well.) If you are writing a major research paper on a relatively well-known artist, the best way to begin is to consult the most recent catalog you can find and to compile as current a bibliography as possible.

The preceding sentence contains two notions about the best ways to begin writing about art that have been implicit assumptions of this text from the outset. First, it is important, especially in the initial stages of writing about art, to begin in the particular. It is far easier to write a paper on *Full Fathom Five* than it is on Jackson Pollock—let alone some even larger topic like "American Abstract Painting, 1940 to the Present." A well-reasoned essay on the particular painting would inevitably lead you to some interesting conclusions about Pollock and about American abstract painting as well.

Second, I have assumed that you do not always have to write a major "research" paper, that much of your writing about art, from essays on examinations to more formal assignments, will depend more on your ability to ask the right questions about works of art. Inevitably, these simpler writings should lead you to a situation where a larger, more ambitious paper might be not merely possible but something you actually want to do. Still, it may not be necessary to consult secondary sources in the library in order to write a good paper about very contemporary or relatively unknown work. If the work refers directly to something you don't know—Shakespeare, say, or a Greek myth—you will have to do a little independent research. But many intelligent papers have been written about art without their authors consulting any sources outside the immediate context of the work itself—its title and label, an accompanying artist's statement, and so on. On the other hand, when you are writing about a relatively well-known work of art or artist, your approach might well benefit from a consideration of the opinions of the larger, well-informed community of scholars and critics. At its best, scholarship in art history can help you to understand the work more fully than you might have without it. At the very least, it should help you to frame the questions with which you will engage the work on your own.

If a major research effort is the order of the day, there are some ways to proceed that will save you time and result in a better paper. If you have the opportunity to write about works of art you can see in person, by all means do so. If you are working from the "museum without walls" (much more likely if you are writing a research paper), if at all possible choose to focus your discussion on one or two particular works. If you must write about some larger topic—if, for instance, you have been asked to write about "a major issue in nineteenth-century art"—then approach the problem *through* three or four particular paintings. In other words, find works that seem to embody in some way the problem at hand, and draw your larger conclusions from a detailed examination of them. There are many advantages to working this way, some of which will be discussed later, but it should be clear that your conclusions will be far more defensible—and seem more sensible—to a reader who has watched you fashion them out of your detailed analysis of particular works.

Research Online

Increasingly, the Internet is revolutionizing the ways in which research and writing are conducted and disseminated. Unless you attend a university with a major research library, probably more information is available to you online than in the library itself. And no matter where you go to school, more *current* information is available online than in print. So thoroughly is the Internet transforming the landscape of information, in fact, that the library, as an institution, is itself being transformed. No longer is the library the "storehouse" of information; it is, rather, a center of access, like the Internet itself, a doorway through which information passes.

By 1997, three-quarters of the college students in the United States were using the Internet to investigate and explore topics of interest and to gather information for research papers.[3] According to Simmons Market Research Bureau, by 2005, 94 percent of college students were using the Internet.[4] In 1992, the world had fifty Web sites; by 2001, it had over 28 million, and as of August 2005, Yahoo claimed to index more than 20 billion documents and images, including over 50 million audio and video files. The sheer scope of the World Wide Web can make it a frustrating place in which to work. So much information is available that unless you are familiar with the best strategies for accessing information, you can easily find yourself mindlessly "surfing" the Web.

Whatever your Web browser—at this writing, Internet Explorer dominates the market (its former rival, Netscape, was shut down at the end of December 2007), although both Safari, developed by Apple, and Firefox, a free and open source browser, are popular—you will want to begin by selecting a keyword search engine to help you explore materials available on the Web. As mentioned in Chapter 1, of all the available search engines, Yahoo! (**http://www.yahoo.com**) and Google (**http://www.google.com**) are probably the most immediately useful to the student of art. One of the very first sites you will discover whichever search engine you use will be Wikipedia (**http://www.wikipedia.org**), which describes itself as a multilingual, web-based, free content encyclopedia founded in 2001. Its over 2 million articles in English are authored and edited by contributors who need not have any specialized knowledge of their subject matter. As a result, while Wikipedia is a reasonable site at which to orient oneself to a subject, it is not particularly reliable. Often, however, Wikipedia will link you to more substantive sites from which you can proceed with your research.

The search engines all have useful help sections that explain the best ways for you to use the program. But remember, they cannot generate synonyms for your keywords, nor can they find something that isn't there. They are increasingly good at recognizing your own misspellings and suggesting an alternate, but they are by no means infallible on this point. It is important to remember that the different search engines use different symbols and words to limit searches. If you were writing a paper on the Roman Colosseum, you might begin by typing in "colosseum." In Google, this would result in over nine million possibilities, including on the first page a board game and a German recording company. You need to limit your search. Searching under "Roman Colosseum" cuts the number down to a still unmanageable but much smaller 177,000. If you are interested in the use of cement in building the Colosseum, you can search "Roman Colosseum Cement" and narrow your search to less than 5,000 possibilities. If you're interested in images only, click "Images" on the Google site, and images available on the Web will be displayed.

Sometimes you will get lucky and arrive immediately at where you want to be. For instance, if you wanted to write on Isamu Noguchi, you would, in almost every search engine, almost immediately locate the Web site of the Isamu Noguchi Garden Museum, an exemplary site designed by Media Farm (**http://www.noguchi.org**). Not only does the site contain a large quantity of superior reproductions of Noguchi's work, in all categories including biomorphic, geometric, stoneworks, portrait heads, paper works, and so on, it contains a collection of his writings, a complete bibliography of works by him and about him, an exhibition history, and two separate biographical surveys, one connecting him to specific times and places he worked, the other to the people with whom he worked. In addition, the Garden Museum site is linked to other relevant sites, including the Noguchi-designed sculpture garden at the Museum of Fine Arts, Houston. There is no better place than such a site to begin your research.

Remember that different search engines catalog different items, and what one lists might or might not be listed in another. Furthermore, not all Web sites are reliable. Determine who is the author or sponsor of the site, information you should be able to find on the site's home page (if there is no link "home" simply erase everything after the first slant-dash in the site's URL address). Consider if the sponsor of the page is just a "fan" or a well-known art historian or museum. Be especially careful if you find information that you are unable to verify elsewhere. And remember, the Internet is constantly in flux. Hundreds, even thousands, of new sites are added daily, just as hundreds disappear. Therefore, it is important for you to *bookmark* (or Hotlist) relevant sites, since search engines constantly modify their lists, and what you found today, you may not be able to find so easily tomorrow. Make a folder in your bookmarks labeled "Art paper" or "Colosseum paper," and whenever you open a site that seems useful, save it in the bookmark folder. Bookmarking will also allow you to manage your time online—browse, bookmark, browse some more, and when you're done browsing you can go back and spend more time at those sites you've bookmarked. Even better, download information from good sites (being sure to note information you will need for documentation, as discussed at the end of this chapter).

Using the Library Catalog and Databases

Research for a good paper can rarely be accomplished on the Web alone. You almost certainly will have to go to the library—in no small part because most if not all of the published scholarship is available only in print or on databases that you can access only at the library. If in your research on the Web you were lucky enough to locate a bibliography, or if, in visiting a museum, you located one in a catalog or artist's statement with a bibliography, begin your research by locating discussions of the one or two works you have chosen to consider in detail in books or journals at the library. If you were writing on van Gogh's *Night Café*, for instance, it would take very little time for you to check the various books on van Gogh in your library for references to the painting. Your library's catalog is probably online. Simply search "Gogh, Vincent van." If you have trouble locating material, that may be because you have focused your subject too narrowly; for instance, *"Night Café"* will probably not have a separate entry or subject heading. If for any reason you have difficulty with a particular search, ask the reference librarian, who will help you locate the subject area heading where you have the best chance of discovering appropriate material. A word of warning: The more contemporary your subject matter, the less likely it is that you will find reference to it in the library's online catalog. You will have to work from magazines and journals and rely on indexes to these reference materials.

If you have access to your library's stacks, you will notice that most of the books on a particular subject have the same general call numbers—usually, two or three related groups. This is because so many books in the art section of the library are grouped in the stacks first by medium, then as subgroups, by nationality, and, finally, within each country, by artist. (If you write very many papers, you will soon get to know which shelves contain what books. You will know where American painting is located, where the sculpture books are, and so on.)

Once you have gathered the basic books on your subject, check their indexes for reference to particular works you want to discuss. If the discussions seem useful or significant, then read them in more detail. Also look at the footnotes to the passages that discuss the works. These might lead you to other important discussions. If a book contains no specific reference to the works in question (some books are badly indexed, and many catalogs are not indexed at all), scan tables of contents and lists of illustrations: Does the book sound interesting anyway? Consider who published the books—a major art book publisher, a university press, a major museum? All of these are some indication of quality. Finally, consider how recently the book was published. The most recent publications will often incorporate and build upon previous scholarship. You can often avoid plowing through much earlier material by reading discussions of it in later publications. If the earlier work seems interesting and important, by all means return to it, but sometimes it will seem, in the light of more recent scholarship, antiquated or irrelevant.

After you have some general notion of how much material there is on the works of art you've chosen to concentrate on, and after you've gotten some sense of the parameters of the critical discussion surrounding them, consult the *Art Abstracts* (previously known as *Art Index*), *BHA* (*Bibliography of the History of Art*), *RAA* (*Répertoire d'art et d'Archeologie*), *RILA* (*Répertoire international de la littérature de l'art*), or all four (though *BHA* subsumed the last two, *RAA* and *RILA* in 1991, and, thus, you will only have to consult the last two for pre-1991 materials). These are basic research tools with which all art students need to be acquainted. They are housed in the reference area of your library. *Art Abstracts* and *BHA* are no longer available in print editions and you will probably access them at your library online—though in some cases your library might own them in CD-ROM format.

Art Abstracts is a year-by-year index of over 370 periodicals published throughout the world. If you were writing on a painting by Jackson Pollock, you would look up "Pollock, Jackson," and there you would find all the articles and essays written about him in the current year back to 1984 (entries before 1984 have yet to be incorporated in the database). Begin at the top of the list, the most current material, and work your way down. Approximately 70 percent of the entries since 1994 include abstracts, or short summaries (not evaluations), of the argument of the book or article. These will help you decide if you want to look at the reference. If there is a lot of writing on your particular subject, then five years ought to be sufficient. If there is very little, you may want to go back for ten years. Just as more recent books tend to incorporate and build upon older scholarship, so do more recent essays in the art journals and magazines. Any important older scholarship will almost certainly be mentioned in the more recent essays. Your library may also subscribe to *Art Full Text*, a more elaborate version of *Art Abstracts* that, in addition to the index and abstract features, provides seamless links to full text articles on any of your library's reference databases.

Art Abstracts offers another important feature. Besides listing each article and essay and giving you some idea of the reproductions accompanying each, it lists by title reproductions of individual works by each artist: What is especially useful is that it also includes reproductions appearing in gallery advertisements and the like. If you are having trouble locating a color reproduction of a work that you've seen only in black and white, you can generally find a color reproduction—if one in fact exists—by patiently working your way back through *Art Abstracts* year by year. Don't forget to check the World Wide Web as well. Recently a distance education student told me that she was able to locate all but one or two of the works of art I discussed in ten weeks of lectures online (that's something over 300 images).

The *BHA* (*Bibliography of the History of Art*) was inaugurated in 1991, merging the *RAA* and *RILA*. These indexes have the disadvantage of covering only post–Classical Western art—*RILA* covers art since the fourth century and *RAA* begins with early Christian art. They exclude non-Western art. The coverage of journals and periodicals in these indexes is, however, sweeping. *BHA* indexes more than 1,750 journals, many of them European. In addition, *BHA* covers books and offers abstracts of all listed materials. These abstracts can be especially useful if your library doesn't subscribe to a given journal or own a particular book. Reading the *BHA* or *RILA* abstract can help you determine how important the material might be to your argument and whether you need to recall it or order it through interlibrary loan.

If you are writing about modern art, you should also consult *ARTbibliographies Modern*, which focuses on work dating from the late nineteenth century onward, including photography since its invention, performance art and installation, video art, computer and electronic art, body art, graffiti, artists' books, and so on. It provides abstracts not only of books and articles, but also exhibition catalogues. The index is available both in a print edition and online.

If you are writing about architecture, you should consult the *Architectural Index*, which you may search by building type, architect/designer, location of building, or a combination of the above. The *Avery Index to Architectural Periodicals* has a more historical focus, containing more than 400,000 entries surveying more than 700 American and international journals, and indexing from 1930 to the present, with selective coverage back to the 1860s. *Art Abstracts* also lists architects and major architectural works.

Another useful online index is the *Arts & Humanities Citation Index*, which contains over 1.4 million records from 1,130 arts and humanities journals. The online version goes back to 1975. Suppose you were writing about Carlo Crivelli's *Crucifixion* (Figure 12), and you began with Joshua C. Taylor's classic discussion of it in *Learning to Look* (see Chapter 2). Because it indexes footnotes and bibliographies from scholarly journals, the *A&HCI* allows you to search for any author who has been cited by other authors. Thus, you could look up Joshua C. Taylor and find a list of all discussions of Taylor's writings.

Increasingly, full-text databases are becoming available. In these, you can read and download an entire article, usually for a fee or by subscription. For instance, if you are interested in reading reviews of important new scholarly art books, articles, exhibitions, conferences, digital and electronic productions, films, videos, and other works, the College Art Association reviews many online at **http://www.caareviews.org**, but membership in the College Art Association is required for access (there are affordable student rates).

No index can ever be completely up-to-date. In print formats, it generally takes at least a couple of years to put together a single volume. Typically, in 2005, you might expect to find indexes covering materials up through 2001, but nothing more recent. The arrival of online databases has diminished the lagtime considerably. But if you need absolutely current material, there is only one thing you can do. You will, at some point late in your research, have a good idea of which journals and magazines show the most interest in your particular subject matter. If you go through the most recent issues of these publications, often you will discover an important piece of recent scholarship.

Using Art Dictionaries and Other Guides

Many times, when you write a more sophisticated paper involving research, you will run across technical vocabulary with which you are unfamiliar. This happens even to the most highly trained art historians and critics. By all means, take the time to look things up you don't know. Your paper will almost always benefit from the extra effort. Ralph Mayer's *Dictionary of Art Terms and Techniques* is an inexpensive paperback reference that is a useful addition to any library. More specialized and complete, though originally published in 1891, the *Adeline Art Dictionary* is an extremely useful summary of specialized terms that are often very well illustrated. It will be housed in the reference section of your library. If you find you need help with terms or concepts that do not appear in *Adeline*, ask your reference librarian.

Originally published in 1996, the 34-volume *Dictionary of Art*, edited by Jane Turner, is now available online as the *Grove Dictionary of Art Online*. A fifteen-year undertaking, with over 41,000 entries, authored by 6,800 scholars from around the world, it is the most inclusive and exhaustive work of its kind. Only film is excluded from its coverage. It includes nearly 20,000 biographies, solid coverage of traditionally neglected areas (photography, the decorative arts, and the art of non-Western peoples), and articles on media, techniques, and schools or groups.

Another useful reference work is James Hall's *Dictionary of Subjects and Symbols in Art*, a guide to classical mythology and religious themes in Western art. If, for instance, you were writing about Carlo Crivelli's *Crucifixion* (Figure 12), you might want to know if there were any special significance to the skull at the foot of the cross. Looking up "skull" in Hall's *Dictionary*, you would find that for "a skull at the foot of the cross, see CRUCIFIXION." Turning to "crucifixion," you would discover that "the skull commonly seen at the foot of the cross . . . represents Adam's own skull," and that this skull "sprinkled with the blood that drips from the Savior's body" is symbolic of the "washing away of Adam's sin."[5] Such information can help you construct a very interesting paper.

Finally, another reference book that is useful to have in your own library and that is available in an inexpensive paperback edition is Peter and Linda Murray's *Dictionary of Art and Artists*, first published in 1959 and revised many times since. It includes short biographies of over 1,200 Western artists.

CONSIDERING THE WORK'S HISTORICAL AND CULTURAL CONTEXT

The largest verbal frame surrounding a work of art—larger even than the body of critical and art historical discussions about it—has to do with its place in the larger scheme of things, art historical and otherwise. Each work is conceived in a particular time and in a particular place, and to some degree it is bound to reflect the circumstances of its conception. Cubism, for instance, developed in Paris between 1907 and 1912 as a group style that defined itself not only in relation to much of the painting that had preceded it—Cézanne's late paintings of Mont Sainte-Victoire were exhibited in 1907 after his death and were very influential—but also in the context of a rapidly developing and changing social milieu.

Between 1890 and the outbreak of World War I in August 1914, the pace of European life was dramatically accelerated, its continuities were disrupted, and its long-held truths undermined. Internal combustion and diesel engines began to power the machines that transported people not only long distances but to their very jobs. Electricity replaced gas light in the streets, and these streets were no longer filled with horses and carriages but, suddenly, with automobiles. In 1900, there were 3,000 automobiles in all of France, but by 1907, that number had jumped to 30,000 and by 1913, France was itself *producing* 45,000 automobiles a year. Henry Adams, visiting the 1900 World's Fair in Paris, looked out across the complex of electric dynamos that powered the Fair, and could only feel that "the planet itself seemed less impressive, in its old-fashioned, de-liberate, annual or daily revolution, than this huge wheel, revolving with-in arm's-length at some vertiginous speed." He found himself, he said, "lying in the Gallery of Machines at the Great Exposition of 1900, with [my] historical neck broken by the sudden irruption of forces totally new."[6] Soon airplanes and zeppelins floated across the Parisian skies. In offices, which a generation earlier had been the realm of scriveners and copyists, the routine of day-to-day business was transformed by the tele-phone, the typewriter, and the tape recorder. The daily newspaper became an institution. Cinemas began to spring up everywhere. In 1905, Einstein published his Special Theory of Relativity, and soon Bohr offered a new model of the atom. As Robert Wohl has put it in an essay on the genera-tion of 1914: "Everything was in flux. Old systems of reference were under attack, old hierarchies were being challenged, and old elites were being pressed to make concessions. Revolution seemed inevitable and those who had something to lose did not conceal their fear."[7] As a style of art, Cubism seemed to embody this upheaval. It reflected, that is, the rapid change and, above all, the "revolutionary" drift of the twentieth century itself. If it was not received with universal enthusiasm, that is be-cause, symbolically at least, it represented the end of one era and the dawn of a new, uncertain future.

The same sorts of context could be, and have been, developed for al-most any recognizable period style. Courbet's realism can be usefully tied to the social upheavals in Europe in 1848, and David's neoclassicism to the French Revolution in 1789. The naturalism that marks Giotto's paint-ing in the early fourteenth century, especially noticeable when compared with the flat, almost abstract medieval formulas for representation that are typical of the painting that precedes him, can be said to inaugurate the Renaissance. Above all, Giotto creates *believable* people, who seem to possess highly personal feelings and a sense of their own individuality. This new "humanism," or interest in the potential and capacity of each in-dividual human being, can be seen throughout Renaissance art, literature, and philosophy. Such "-isms" are the lens through which we interpret works of art. They are systems or doctrines of artistic practice and philo-sophical belief that characterize the work of a period or group.

The more you know about a given period, the more easily you will be able to place whatever works of art you are discussing from that peri-od within a larger context. For this reason, my university requires art his-tory students to take a sequence of courses on the history of Western civilization either before or concurrently with the Survey of Western Art sequence; I often advise students registering for, say, Nineteenth-Century

French Painting to take a course concurrently in nineteenth-century French history or literature.

In the end, however, you will do far better to define, in your paper, the particular qualities that contribute to the power and interest of, for instance, *Full Fathom Five*, than to try to fit *Full Fathom Five* into some preconceived notion of American abstract expressionism or the history of post–World War II American culture. There are, for one thing, widely varying ideas about what, precisely, abstract expressionism even is, let alone how it came to be the most important art movement in the world in the 1950s. One school of thought sees it as a kind of painting interested only in painting for its own sake—"pure painting," as Pollock himself put it. For this point of view, his greatest paintings are the numbered works of 1947–1950, which have no overt reference.

A second group sees abstract expressionism as the record of an event—the painting becomes the record, as it were, of Pollock's physical and mental activity. Still others are interested in the way the idea of representation seems to be contested in the paintings, and this group is especially interested in Pollock's inclusion of more representational elements under layers of paint, as if he is repressing them. This final insight, furthermore, offers those who would like to read Pollock's painting in psychoanalytic terms a way to deal with it from yet another perspective.[8] Which, you ask, is the best approach to *Full Fathom Five*? If you're like me, you're tempted to like something in both of them, but the point is, there are many different approaches to the same work of art, each offering a particular set of insights into the work.

In recent years, some of the most important contributions to our understanding of works of art have come from our increased awareness of their place in **social history**. That is, rather than just considering the formal and stylistic aspects of a work of art, issues such as race, class, gender, and ideology are considered in relation to the work. How, the question is asked, does the work of art reflect broader social patterns of belief and behavior?

Consider, for instance, a sculptural figure from the Kongo of a type first made for centuries to cure illness, ward off evil, or punish wrongdoers (Figure 32). This is an example of one made after the imposition of colonial rule in the nineteenth century, a *nkisi nkonde* (plural *minkisi minkonde*). Throughout Central Africa, all significant human powers are believed to result from communication with the dead. A *nkisi* (meaning "sacred medicine") is any one of a number of different varieties of magical figures through which certain ritual specialists—healers, diviners, defenders of the living—can communicate with the spirit world and obtain the power to act effectively on earth. The most formidable of *minkisi* is the

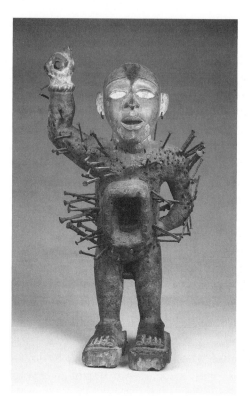

Figure 32   Magical figure, *nikisi nkonde*, Kongo (Muserongo), Zaire, late nineteenth century. Wood, iron nails, glass, resin, height 20 in. The Stanley Collection. X1986.573. The University of Iowa Museum of Art, Iowa City, IA.

variety known as *minkonde*, pictured here, figures believed to pursue witches, thieves, adulterers, and evildoers—including colonial forces—by night. *Minkonde* figures generally stand upright, holding a spear in one raised arm, ready to attack. (The spear is missing here, but would have been inserted through the round hole in the figure's raised hand.) The box-like hole in the figure's stomach is designed to hold magical substances—most often kaolin, a white clay believed to be closely linked to the world of the dead, and red ochre, linked symbolically to blood. The powers of the *nkisi nkonde* are activated when the individual who possesses it drives nails, blades, and other pieces of iron into it, believing that similar injuries will be incurred by those whom the *nkisi nkonde* seeks out and punishes.

Christian missionaries and colonial soldiers who encountered such figures in the nineteenth and early twentieth centuries were completely unaware of the social and cultural role they played in Kongo society. They associated their ferocious appearance with witchcraft and devil worship, a view exacerbated when Kongo peoples quite naturally associated the nails in the *minkonde* figures with the nails fixing Christ to the cross in the crucifixion. European military commanders, not altogether incorrectly, saw such figures as evidence of an aggressive native opposition to colonial rule. Missionaries and military commanders confiscated the *minkonde* figures, and destroyed many of them. They did not understand that the figures represented a form of *animism*, the belief in the existence of souls, and that nonhuman things, such as sculptures, can also be endowed with a soul.

When we ask in what ways works of art reflect broader social patterns of belief and behavior, many other questions might arise as well. **Feminist art criticism**, for instance, has been particularly effective at drawing attention to the ways in which Western art has codified and institutionalized the male gaze as the preeminent point of view. This is explicit in Albrecht Dürer's *Draftsman Drawing a Reclining Nude*, from *The Art of Measurement* (Figure 33), although it may not have seemed so to Dürer. From Dürer's point of view, the object of the artist's study presents a formal problem, not a social one. But this is precisely the point: the artist's gaze turns woman into an object—something called, in the classic texts, "form." The grid through which he views her does not just allow him to draw her accurately—his eye suspended over a strikingly phallic obelisk—but it allows him to "master" her. She is nude and vulnerable; he clothed and strong. She passively submits herself to his gaze; his gaze actively controls and dominates her body. She is defined as something to be looked at; he as the centered, focused, subject around whom the world turns.

In other words, one of the strategies of the "masculinist" gaze is to transform the very idea of vision into a question of form. Arguably, Dürer is objectively rendering what he sees before his eyes. In Western art, we tend to privilege vision as the measure of certainty and truth (think, for

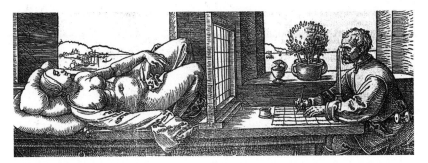

Figure 33 Albrecht Dürer, *Draftsman Drawing a Reclining Nude,* from *The Art of Measurement*, c. 1527. Woodcut, 3 in. × 8½ in. Courtesy of Museum of Fine Arts, Boston, Horatio Greenough Curtis Fund. © 2005 Museum of Fine Arts, Boston. All rights reserved.

instance, of the authority eye-witness accounts have in legal disputes). But, as our reading of the Dürer suggests, other truths may be at work in the ostensibly neutral ground that lies between the observer and the observed. I have, for instance, read Georgia O'Keeffe's charcoal drawing *Alligator Pears in a Basket* (Figure 15) as a study in light and dark—in other words, in purely formal terms. By not recognizing in the work another, more female content—the basket can be seen as a metaphor for the womb, containing and holding its ripening fruit—it could be argued that I have subjected it to precisely this male gaze. Similarly, I have ignored the apparent weakness of the male figure in Käthe Kollwitz's *The Downtrodden* (Figure 16), and I have seen in Picasso's *Woman with Book*, reproduced on the back cover, a harmony of colors where perhaps I ought to recognize their dissonance, a loving gaze where perhaps it is better to feel a more threatening force. As Arianna Stassinopoulos Huffington reminds us in her biography, *Picasso: Creator and Destroyer*: "What seemed a life guided by burning passions—for painting, for women, for ideas—seemed a moment later the story of a man unable to love, intent on seduction not in the search for love, not even in the desire to possess, but in a compulsion to destroy."[9] In Huffington's view, the figure in the mirror behind Marie-Thérèse becomes more ominous. The point is a simple one: The feminist perspective offers exciting possibilities for us to re-see and reinterpret works of art.

The male gaze proscribed in feminist criticism is the same gaze that colonized the world in the eighteenth and nineteenth centuries—the "master's gaze," which oppressed people of color, asserted the ascendancy of Western civilization, and, at best, viewed people unlike itself as the exotic or "other." The reaction of Europeans to the Kongolese *minkisi minkonde* is an example. The dominant way of seeing the world—and in some sense, therefore, the *only* way to see the world, since it was the only one that was *recognized*—was white, Western, and male. These are precisely the terms that have defined race relations in the United States, where the institution of slavery subjected African Americans to the "master's gaze" from the outset. Many African-American artists have sought to re-see the African-American experience from their own point of view, and perhaps one of the most powerful of these explorations can be found in the work of Kara Walker. Walker's principlal medium is the silhouette, a form of art that originated in the courts of Europe in the early eighteenth century. Its most famous practitioner, from whom the practice gets its name, was Etienne de Silhouette. Silhouette served as minister of Finance to the court of the French king, Louis XV, whose ruthless taxation of the French people, together with his almost total distain for their plight, would lead to revolution in 1789.

Walker's silhouettes translate the social and political origins of the art form—the class conflict at its core—into the context of slavery in the antebellum South. *Insurrection!*, a detail of which is pictured here (Figure 34), is a room-size installation that unfolds across three walls. Light projectors from the ceiling throw light across the room, projecting the viewers' shadows onto the walls, so that they themselves become active silhouettes in the scene. Here slaves disembowel a plantation owner with a soup ladle as another readies to strike him with a frying pan. At the left, yet another slave raises her fist in defiance—*Our Tools Were Rudimentary*, reads the subtitle, *Yet We Pressed On.*

Examining the cultural and historical context of art offers some of the most exciting possibilities for writing about art. Bring your other coursework in the university to bear on what you study in art history. Think about the ways in which your history course, or your sociology course, might inform the artworks you see. Such perspectives can only challenge your own assumptions about the work of art, and every time you challenge an assumption, greater understanding is the only result.

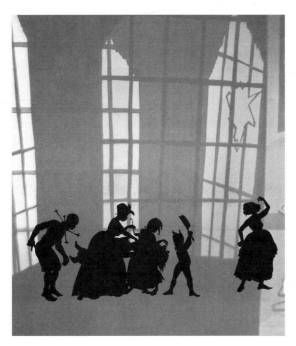

Figure 34   Kara Walker, *Insurrection! (Our Tools Were Rudimentary, Yet We Pressed On)*, installation view, 2000. Cut paper silhouettes and light projections, site-specific dimensions. Solomon R. Guggenheim Museum, New York. Purchased with funds contributed by the International Director's Council and Executive Committee Members, 2000. Photo: Ellen Labenski. © Solomon R. Guggenheim Museum, New York.

QUOTING AND DOCUMENTING YOUR SOURCES

Learning the Art of Quoting

The greatest danger that students confront when they write research papers is that their final paper will contain, in the end, nothing of their own but will be a compendium of appropriate quotations. This is as true, incidentally, of doctoral students as it is first-year undergraduates. Many a doctoral thesis is overburdened by references. It is a failing that is easy to understand: Why speak for yourself when so many people more informed than yourself can speak for you? And besides, you want the professor to see how much research you've done. Remember, however, that it is *your* mind that the professor wants to see at work, not that of some famous critic.

Here is a rule of thumb for fitting quotations into your own writing: *When you quote, always move on from the quotation and continue the paragraph by developing the idea the quotation initiates.*

Earlier in this chapter it was suggested that you approach critical essays in the spirit of initiating a dialogue with them. By forcing yourself to respond to the material you quote, you will in fact begin just such a dialogue. You will never become a slave to your research. Also, in a very real sense, by responding to it and developing it further, you will make the quoted material your own. It becomes part of your argument, not something outside your argument to which you have deferred.

In other words, there is a real art to quoting. You want to quote things that are especially informative or well written. Such material tends to elevate the quality of your own prose. As in playing tennis, you tend to play to the level of your opposition; this is not to say, however, that you should quote only opinions with which you can argue. Some of the best passages in papers are those in which something is said well in a quotation and then the student, in the particular context of the argument at hand, says it better. Perhaps you have noticed that in this book other critics have been quoted precisely in this way. Joshua Taylor's discussion of the Perugino and Crivelli crucifixions cited in Chapter 2 is a classic piece of art historical writing. I have tried to elevate my own discussion by incorporating Taylor's argument into my own, but I built on Taylor's distinctions, and I used them to my own ends. The discussion of Perugino and Crivelli was developed, in fact, to provide you with a model for quoting authoritative sources. Refer to it when you want to quote secondary sources (and be sure to note that the quotation furthers an argument that continues after the quotation itself). Refer also to the technical discussions of quotation and ellipses, in Sections 14 and 15 of the Appendix. Good writing tends to stimulate more good writing. When you read criticism, look not only for useful information but also for the well-turned phrase, the interesting and informative anecdote, the particularly insightful analysis of a work of art. These things can do more than inform you, they can provide a foundation upon which to build your own essay.

Acknowledging Your Sources

I am constantly surprised at the number of students who seem to be embarrassed that they have consulted research materials. To the contrary, doing so shows energy, interest, and determination. The only times you need to worry about using such materials—except when the professor, for whatever reason, asks you not to consult secondary sources—is when you have done a superficial job, consulting only one or two books or articles and, more important, when you have not acknowledged that you have done so. If you do research, do it well. If you appropriate phrases, whole passages, ideas—even if you've put these in your own words—or the logic of an argument from someone else, and you fail to acknowledge it, then you have plagiarized the work. The penalties for plagiarism vary from school to school, but they are never very pleasant.

If you use research materials well—as the beginning of your argument, not as an end in themselves—then you need never be embarrassed to cite these materials. In fact, one of the checks you can use to judge the quality of your own paper is to determine at the draft stage just how much of *you* there is in the paper. If you detect more of your absence from the argument than your presence, if you feel that one solution might be to go back and convert some quotations into your own words, then you have probably not entered into a dialogue with the criticism so much as let the criticism rule you. To revise, engage the criticism. See if you can push its ideas further, perhaps by using it to analyze a particular work, a work with which it hasn't dealt.

You do not need to footnote or acknowledge anything that could be considered common knowledge—dates of birth and death, the location of paintings, historical facts, the definitions of words, and so on. Generally, if a question of interpretation seems to enter into the material, or if the fact seems genuinely new, then by all means cite your source. When in doubt, play it safe. But again, watch for over-citation. If you consistently have more than two or three footnotes per typed page, then something is wrong—either you are acknowledging things you need not acknowledge or your argument is too dependent on outside sources.

Choosing Your Footnote Style

Footnote conventions in art history differ widely, and as you read you will encounter many different styles. They depend, among other things, on where the article or book you are reading was published. The British have one system; the Americans another. Even in the United States, conventions differ from publication to publication: *Art in America* has its own ideas about what a footnote should look like, while the *Art Bulletin* has a completely different set of standards.

The footnotes that have been used in this book should give you an idea of the style suggested by *The Chicago Manual of Style*, a style preferred by many book publishers. In all styles, however, a few general rules apply. Generally, in order to designate a footnote, simply put a raised number after the final punctuation of the sentence, unless there are several references in a single sentence (something you should work to avoid), or unless clarity demands that you footnote a single phrase in an otherwise complex sentence (something else that you can probably avoid). Number the notes consecutively and, if you are typing, put them at the end of the paper (it is simply too difficult to put footnotes at the bottom of the page if you are typing). If you are using a word processor, you can probably choose whether to put them at the end of the paper or at the bottom of the page. Some people prefer notes at the bottom of the page, some at the back of the paper. Ask your professor. However, if you put your footnotes at the end of the paper, do *not* staple the pages together, since the professor will probably want to remove them and consult them while reading the paper. Many people prefer that notes be double-spaced to facilitate reading and corrections. Again, ask about this.

Each footnote citation is, in effect, a one-sentence paragraph. Indent, type the number, and then type the footnote. It will begin with a capital letter and end with a period. Outlined in the following pages are two alternative styles for your consideration.

The Chicago Style.   Briefly, for citations of a **book**, the Chicago Style form is the following:

1. Author(s), *Title* (Place of publication: Publisher, date of publication), page numbers.

The author's name appears in its normal sequence—given name, initials, and surname—followed by a comma. The title is italicized, or underlined to indicate italics if you do not have access to italic type. There is no punctuation between the title and the parenthesis (never place a comma before parenthesis, in footnotes or otherwise), but a comma follows the parenthetical information. Finally, the page numbers are listed, without the abbreviations "p." or "pp." The note ends with a period. Thus, if you were to refer to these two pages in this book, your note, following the style outlined above, would look like this:

1. Henry M. Sayre, *Writing About Art* (Upper Saddle River, NJ: Prentice Hall, 2005), 88–89.

If there is an **editor** or **translator** to the edition you are using, follow the title with a comma and place that information before the parenthetical information, again followed by no punctuation, as in the tenth note to Chapter 1 in this book:

10. André Malraux, *Museum Without Walls*, trans. Stuart Gilbert and Francis Price (London: Secker & Warburg, 1967), 11–12.

The abbreviation "trans." is usually employed for "translated by," and "ed." for "edited by."

There are two special instances of citation that often come up in writing about art. Sometimes you will be quoting from a recent edition of a classic text, but it will seem important, for clarity's sake, that you acknowledge in the note the original publication date of the text. Perhaps you are writing about art history in the 1950s, and you cite Kenneth Clark's 1953 Mellon Lectures on the nude, first published in 1956, but the edition you are using was published by Princeton University Press in the 1970s. Use the following form:

2. Kenneth Clark, *The Nude: A Study in Ideal Form* (1956; rpt. Princeton, NJ: Princeton University Press, 1972), 56.

Here, the abbreviation "rpt." means "reprinted by."

The second special case involves secondhand references. You want to quote material that you have discovered not in the original work but quoted by someone else. In this case, use a double citation:

3. Henri Matisse, *Jazz* (Paris: Verve, 1947), unpaginated; quoted in John Elderfield, *Henri Matisse: A Retrospective* (New York: Museum of Modern Art, 1992), 23.

Here, the first part of the citation is separated from the second half by a semicolon. If you are quoting from text that does not give you any information about the source of the original, you may want to begin your citation with the phrase "Quoted in."

In order to refer to an article or essay in a **journal** or **magazine**, use this form:

4. Author(s), "Title of Article," *Name of Journal* Vol # (Date of publication): page number(s).

An essay that is included in an **anthology** of essays begins in the same way, but then is treated like a book:

5. Author(s), "Title of Essay," *Name of Anthology*, ed. Name of editor (Place of publication: Publisher, date of publication), page number(s).

In both cases, the title of the article or essay is in quotation marks and the name of the journal or book is italicized (or underlined to indicate italics if you are typing). In the case of the article in a journal or magazine, there is no punctuation either between the journal name and the volume number or between the volume number and the date of publication (except the parenthesis). The date of publication is put in parentheses and is followed by a colon. The page numbers, again, are not introduced by "p." or "pp." If there are no page numbers, as there often are not in art publications, simply put "unpaginated." The following is an example from the footnotes at the back of this book:

5. Brian O'Doherty, "Inside the White Cube: Notes on the Gallery Space," *Artforum* 14 (March 1976): 24–25.

When you make **subsequent references** to a work you've already cited in full, you may shorten your note. For instance, a subsequent reference to the article above might look like this:

6. O'Doherty, 25.

If there were more than one article by O'Doherty cited in your text, you would lengthen the note in order to avoid confusion:

6. O'Doherty, "Inside the White Cube," 25.

When the note refers to exactly the same citation as the one that precedes it, it is still permissible to use the Latin abbreviation "Ibid.," short for *ibidem*, "in the same place." I actually prefer it, since it is perfectly clear, and shortens the notes. For instance, if note 7 were also to O'Doherty's "Inside the White Cube," and to the same page, your note would be:

7. Ibid.

If it were to a different page, however, it would be:

7. Ibid., 29.

If you do a lot of writing, you might want to purchase the *Chicago Manual* (more than just a footnote guide, it is a complete guide to style and usage), but the reference desk in almost every library will have a copy of it. For difficult footnote problems, consult it. Almost every imaginable contingency is anticipated.

The Art Bulletin Style. A second possible footnote style is that of the *Art Bulletin*, among the most prestigious of the art history journals. It differs considerably from the Chicago Style. It is what as known as a "short form" method of citation (the full references will appear in your bibliography). Any citation of a text that is referred to frequently in the essay consists only of the author's surname and the page number, separated by a comma, even in the first citation (in this case, imagine I am citing Linda Nochlin's *Realism*):

1. Nochlin, 243.

If there are two or more books by Nochlin cited in your text, they are distinguished by a short abbreviation of the title, and Nochlin's full name is included with an abbreviation of the title in the form of an initial:

1. Linda Nochlin, R, 243. (R is for *Realism*.)

2. Linda Nochlin, WAP, 15. (WAP is for *Women, Art, and Power*.)

Two or more articles by the same author are cited by name and year of publication (the full references will appear in your bibliography):

1. Hickey, 1997, 60.

2. Hickey, 1995, 80.

If two or more articles by the author have the same year of publication, they should be designated by "a," "b," "c," and so on:

1. Hickey, 1997a, 114.

As in the Chicago Style, "Ibid." replaces "Nochlin" if the reference is to the work cited in the immediately preceding note.

Works not cited frequently in the essay employ a more extended footnote form. For books, use the following format:

2. Henry M. Sayre, *Writing About Art*, Upper Saddle River, NJ, 1999, 77–78.

Notice that this form is an abbreviated version of the Chicago Style. No publisher is listed, and parentheses are not utilized. For articles, use the following format:

5. Brian O'Doherty, "Inside the White Cube: Notes on the Gallery Space," *Artforum*, XIV, March 1976, 24–25.

Again, no parentheses are utilized. The volume number of the journal is indicated in this format by roman numerals. Second references to infrequently cited sources refer to the first citation:

7. O'Doherty (as in n. 5), 27.

The "short form" may seem far less cumbersome at first glance, but it requires a bibliography of all frequently cited sources at the end of the essay. The citations are listed in alphabetical order by author. Here are representative examples:

Nochlin, Linda, R: *Realism*, New York, 1971.

_____, WAP: *Women, Art, and Power and Other Essays*, New York, 1988.

Hickey, Dave, 1995, "Edward Ruscha: *Twentysix Gasoline Stations, 1962*," *Artforum*, XXXIII, Summer, 80–81, 126.

_____, 1997, "Critical Encounters," *Artforum*, XXXV, January, 60–61.

Notice, in these examples, that the second listing of works by the same author is indicated with an extended underline (five spaces). The abbreviation used for book titles follows the author's name, followed by a colon. In the case of articles, the date has been moved forward after the author's name to help distinguish more quickly between works.

It is useful to keep in mind that footnote styles are not meant to confuse you, though they almost inevitably seem diabolically complicated to most beginning writers. They are meant to be straightforward references for your reader's information and convenience. There is, in the end, a very easy set of principles that can guide you in developing your notes: After the first full citation, be as brief as your sense of clarity will allow, be logical, and be consistent. If you err, err in the direction of providing too much information. If you feel confusion set in, get help from the *Chicago Manual* or consult a recent issue of the *Art Bulletin*.

Citing Internet Sources

Conventions for citing Internet sources are constantly changing as the Internet continuously develops, but a few principles are by now clear. As with books and articles, you need to cite author and title if available, and then the URL (Universal Resource Locator, the unique Internet address of a given document) of the site itself. You also need to cite the date you visited the site. Sites on the World Wide Web are subject to constant update and change. As a result, something you cite today may well have been modified later, moved to a different location, or even disappeared. Web pages all possess a "last modified" date, which will allow anyone looking for the material in your citation to see if the site has been revised since you visited it.

To cite a document available on the World Wide Web, you must minimally use the following form:

1. Author(s), "Title of document," original source if available, *Title of the Website*, Website host, date the site was posted (if available, otherwise write "n.d.," no date), <URL> (date of visit).

1. Isamu Noguchi, "On Gardens as Sculpture," from *A Sculptor's World* (New York: Harper Row, 1968), The Noguchi Museum, n.d., <www.noguchi.org/intextall.html#gardens> (18 Mar. 1998).

To cite an **e-mail** communication, use the following form:

1. Author <author's e-mail address> "subject line from posting," date of communication, type of communication [i.e., personal communication, distribution list, or Listserv address in angle brackets] (date of access).

1. Jackson Flash <jackflash@rock.com> "Re: Jumping," 16 Feb. 1998, personal communication (19 Feb. 1998).

Note that the URL or e-mail address in each case is contained within brackets: <URL> ore <e-mail address>. This avoids any confusion, such as including the period at the end of the citation as part of the URL or address.

An increasingly popular form of art writing online are the art blogs. "Blog" is short for "weblog" and refers to an online journal to which its author contributes on a daily or weekly basis. Most blogs invite reader comments and serve as online forums. Among the most popular of the art blogs, although its author, Washington, DC writer Tyler Green, does not generally post reader comments, is *Modern Art Notes* (**http://artsjournal.com/man**). Green's monthly readership is about 90,000, and one of its most useful features is the large number of links to other current art-related material on the Internet. To cite Green's blog, use the following form:

 1. Author, "Blog entry title," date of blog entry, *Title of Blog* <URL> (date of visit).

 1. Tyler Green, "Museum Attendence by Federal Agents Up Dramatically," 25 Jan. 2008, *Modern Art Notes* http://artsjournal.com/man> (26 Jan. 2008).

The title of the blog cited here gives something of the flavor of Green's blog—it's a story about federal agents serving search warrants to several Los Angeles area museums for smuggling antiquities.

A comment posted to a blog poses a more detailed citation:

 1. Comment posted by author [often a pseudonym], date of comment, responding to Author, "Blog entry title," date of blog entry, *Title of Blog* <URL> (date of visit).

 1. Comment posted by "ace," 21 Jan 2008, responding to Arcy Douglas, "What the Portland Art Center Closing Means to Me," 20 Jan. 2008, *PORT* <http://www.portlandart.net> (25 Jan. 2008).

The Web is a fluid and ever-changing space, and it may require you to be inventive in citing it. Simply be sure you have entered all the information needed by others to locate your source for themselves.

4

WORKING WITH WORDS AND IMAGES

The Process of Writing
About What You See

You can begin the actual process of writing about a particular work of art in many ways. Once you've chosen what you're going to discuss, once you've looked at it carefully for a while, the point comes when you must put pen to paper—or, as is often the case these days, open a new file in your software—and begin. Many people never fully discover what it is they think until they begin to write. The process of writing in itself can free you to articulate what you think. Being forced to write something down sometimes helps you to make up your mind.

GATHERING TOGETHER WHAT YOU KNOW

Taking Notes in a Gallery or Museum

The process of writing should begin as early as possible—from the moment you are assigned a topic or from the first moment you enter a gallery or museum. When you visit a gallery or museum, jot down your feelings, your initial impressions, which painting or sculpture attracts you. You might even want to note which items seem totally uninteresting. Then give yourself a chance, later, to see if these apparently "uninteresting" works are still with you. If they are, there might be something more to them than you originally thought, something worth investigating and developing. Above all, don't suppose that you will remember how you felt, that you will be able to recreate the process of choices and decisions that finally leads you to your interest in a particular work. When I review exhibitions or shows, I first quickly tour the gallery or exhibition space, taking notes, diagramming the rooms, noting what intrigues me, what alienates me, and what seems less than important. Depending on the show, I might jot down titles, dates, the names of painters. If I quickly recognize a direction of thought I want to pursue, I'll make notes about that. If I find any exceptional highlights, works around which I sense I could focus a discussion, I'll write those down as well.

Then I leave. I go out to the lobby, or to a restaurant, or to a nearby park bench, and reread my notes. In a short time I have a pretty good sense of what I need to go back to see. I make notes about possible lines of thought to pursue, questions that seem to be raised, works I need to look at more intently. I generally try to ask myself a couple of questions that will force me to consider works I might otherwise ignore. I might even jot down in my notebook—and I have done it—how could anybody (i.e., the curator or the painter or whomever) interested in "x" (which I like) also be interested in "y" (which I don't)? I'll look at all those things I don't like in order to see what, if any, redeeming qualities I can discover in them.

This process doesn't take a very long time. I usually like to make a quick short visit before lunch, followed by a more leisurely and more intense viewing afterward. I almost always have a good sense of what I want to say, and which works I want to focus my discussion on, within a half hour of my return visit. Then the real work of writing begins.

Taking Notes As You Read

After a gallery visit, I will usually begin to read about the work or works that interest me. I may have purchased a catalogue at the museum, or picked up a brochure. I may go online and look for the Web site of a contemporary artist. Eventually, I will get to the library. All along, I will be taking notes on what I read.

As a student, very often you will begin here, since you may well not have the opportunity to go to a museum or gallery, or the work or works you are writing about are in a museum too far away for you to visit. Here are some general rules to keep in mind as you read and take notes:

1. If you own the book you are reading, underline or highlight key ideas and arguments as you read, and jot down brief reactions to the material in the margins. It is, however, important to keep track of these ideas. I find it useful to group major issues or themes for quick reference on the

blank pages at the back or front of the book. So, for instance, at the back of my copy of Arthur Danto's *After the End of Art*, I have written the following:

> *Danto's argument—xiii, 4, 198*
> *the modernist narrative—7–8*
> *on exhibitions—169*

In essence, these references amount to a personal index, allowing me to quickly retrieve the material I find most useful or interesting in Danto's book. Do not underline too heavily—restrict yourself to the well-turned phrase or the well-stated idea. And do not underline or highlight any book you do not own.

2. If you have found a useful discussion in a journal, it is generally a good idea to photocopy it so that you can highlight and annotate the article. Be sure that you take down all the needed bibliographic information and note it on the photocopy, and be sure that the page numbers are visible (photocopiers often cut off the margins of the original).

3. Highlighting does not take the place of note-taking. You need not copy highlighted material onto a note card or into your computer (I personally take notes in the Notebook feature in Microsoft Word's Project Gallery). But you do need to create a separate handwritten note card or computer note page referring to the material you've highlighted in your reading. For example, the note card for Danto's commentary on exhibitions might look like this:

Danto on exhibitions, Art After the End of Art, 169

You need this reference so that when you later sit down to write your paper, you can shuffle your notes into the order that you will address them in your paper. In effect, organizing your notes amounts to the first draft of your paper.

4. Put any material that you copy directly from a source in quotation marks, citing the source, so that you later know with certainty that this material is not your own. Whenever you do quote, try to react to the quotation on your note card. My note page citing Danto on exhibitions reads in its entirety:

> *Danto on exhibitions, Art After the End of Art, 169*
>
> *—explaining, in large part, the popularity of the retrospective exhibition in the late 20th century.*

In other words, when I review my notes, I know why I want to quote Danto on exhibitions and how his thinking fits into my general argument.

In the same way, when I copied the passage from Brian O'Doherty's "Inside the White Cube" into my notes in preparing to write his book (see page 11), I wrote: "But the work always must meet up with us—it's not free!" The moment I wrote this in my notes, I knew exactly how and where I would use O'Doherty in this book.

5. Above all, taking notes is an exercise in critical thinking. Remember, your paper is not a place to regurgitate others' ideas. Rather, your own independent thinking should build upon the thinking of others. In fact, if you are thinking critically, you should accumulate, as you read, several note cards that represent nothing but your own thinking.

FOCUSING YOUR DISCUSSION

If you read many discussions about art, you will quickly notice that the most readable and interesting of them almost always focus on particular works. If you go back and look at whatever section of this book has seemed to you the most interesting, you will probably find that it is a particular discussion of a particular work. In other words, I could discuss something like color theory all day on a fairly abstract level, but what makes it interesting, in the end, is van Gogh's particular application of a complementary color scheme in *The Night Café* and Picasso's in *Woman with Book*. Similarly, as a writing tactic, for the discussion in the last chapter I tried to find an interesting example of a work whose title and medium both mattered, Pollock's *Full Fathom Five*, in order to sustain your interest (and in order to be convincing). Consider how dry the previous chapters might have been without particular examples and sometimes highly detailed analysis. Then consider how likely you would have been to get much out of them without those examples.

In other words, this art textbook, like many others, is organized by the principle of using extended discussions of particular works to make more general points. When art appreciation or art history professors analyze works of art in class, they are usually providing you with the same sorts of models. Ground your writing in the concrete discussion of particular works. Focus on the specific problems of form, design, and content that they raise. You will almost always discover that in the process of describing and analyzing particular works, you will arrive at more general conclusions that you did not anticipate.

What are the advantages of writing in this way? In the first place, when you begin to write, you do not know precisely where you are going, what your conclusions will be. This approach to writing does run somewhat counter to the rationale of outline making. Outlines have their function—they provide a way for you to organize your ideas and present them in an orderly way—but if you let order supplant inspiration so that you find yourself filling out the skeleton of your outline to the necessary 1,000 or 2,000 words, then both the process of writing your essay and the essay itself will be boring. Often I can look at a group of student essays and tell who worked from outlines from the outset and who didn't. The giveaway is that in an essay first conceived in outline form, the introduction and the conclusion are almost always virtually the same. A skilled writer will manage to alter the language a little, but the substance will not change. This occurs because, as the writer begins, the essay's conclusions are already predetermined. In contrast, an essay that begins as a process of discovery and exploration, as an exercise in critical thinking, almost always ends differently than it begins. It discovers something it didn't anticipate. It articulates connections it could at first only intuit. The second kind of essay is almost always more interesting to read. It seems to be engaged. It seems active, whereas the other kind of essay, no matter how "right" it might be, seems static in comparison.

To outline effectively and avoid being trapped in a predetermined set of assumptions, think of your main and subordinate ideas as opportunities to ask questions. If you were to write about Pollock's *Full Fathom Five*, you might begin your outline like this:

I. What is the significance of the title?
   A. What is the reference to Shakespeare and what does he mean?
      1. Idea of death
      2. Idea of transformation (i.e., "sea-change")
      3. What is the connection between death and transformation?
   B. How do Shakespeare's themes relate to Pollock's technique?
      1. All-over effect of canvas (i.e., abstraction)
      2. Submergence of recognizable objects in paint
      3. What has suffered a sea-change here? Representation?
II. The idea of surface and depth, etc.
      1. If the surface is abstraction, what lies beneath it?
      2. What are the painting's "depths"?
      3. Might they be psychological?
      4. So what does the title finally imply?

These questions, of course, are not easy to answer, and though you might have some idea of the direction in which you need to go after having arrived at the outline, the territory remains relatively uncharted and interesting to explore. Perhaps, above all, this outline initiates a process of critical thinking, one that gives you the opportunity to explore.

Whether or not you choose to outline beforehand, during the revision process, you can check the logical development of your essay by seeing if you are able to outline your argument. For the many writers who find outlining an overly restrictive way to begin writing, other ways to begin are available. Depending on your temperament, any of the methods described in the next sections, or some combination of them, perhaps even including outlining, might suit you.

Brainstorming and Mapping

I began to organize this book by brainstorming. In other words, I made a random list of topics and subjects that I thought I should address in a book on writing about art. This is how the list began:

formal elements	indexes
principles of design	footnote form
the museum	the verbal frame
the museum without walls	words and images
the "white cube"	Weems's *Coffee Pot*
Duchamp's urinal	student essays
Joshua Taylor	outlining, prewriting, etc.
titles	revising

For several days I added to this list, and as I did so, certain patterns began to emerge. Some of these patterns were evident from the outset; for instance, a cluster of ideas about museums seemed important right away. Soon the titles of the four chapter headings presented themselves. I began to fill out the list in greater detail, grouping elements as I went. For instance, the phrase "the verbal frame" suggested a group of ideas for more particular development:

the "verbal frame" } Pollock's *Full Fathom Five*
importance of title
importance of medium

A whole page began to take shape under the heading "formal elements." I listed each formal element separately and jotted down ideas about how I might approach it:

Line
—Taylor on crucifixions
—use later to talk about quotation (?)
—leads to discussion of space/perspective
—Monet's *Gare St.-Lazare*

I eventually discarded many ideas that occurred to me. A great many notations, followed by question marks, alerted me to places where I might tie discussions together. Some of these I followed up, some I never did. New ideas and modifications continued to occur to me throughout the writing process. Nevertheless, the essential drift of this book was in place in a matter of a few weeks.

Mapping is a more visual form of this method of planning an essay, one that many art students find particularly appealing. A partial map of the section on the formal elements in this book would look like the chart at the top of the next page. Begin by writing your subject in a circle at the center of a sheet of paper. Draw a line out from the circle and name a major subdivision of your subject. Circle it and move out again from there to further subdivisions. You can include possible illustrations and examples, make notes about connections to yourself, even, if your paper is large enough, jot down a few key sentences and ideas on the margins of the map.

Rearranging and organizing notes is a form of mapping. Imagine each circle as a pile of note cards—several quoting Joshua Taylor on Perugino and Crivelli, several others containing ideas about Monet's *Gare Saint-Lazare*, still others on Franz Kline. All these cards might be organized one after the other, in the order to be discussed. As you arrange your notes, new ideas may well occur to you. Don't trust yourself to remember these ideas. Jot down a new note, and put it in your note card "map."

Most of you will not be faced with taking on a project as large as writing a book, but the approaches described above are useful even if you have to write only a short paper. Furthermore, if you find outlining useful, brainstorming and mapping are very good tools for generating your outline. It should be obvious that the material on "Line" above is really an informal outline, the beginnings of the much more formal shape the section of "Line" in this book would eventually take.

Using Prewriting As a Way to Begin

One way to begin your essay, as suggested at the end of Chapter 2, is to describe the work of art in some detail. Some students are more comfortable, at least initially, writing in a looser, somewhat more freewheeling style than the more systematic approach of the formal description. There are no rules in prewriting. Anything goes. The object, in fact, is to put down on paper as much as you can think of in a relatively limited amount of time. A lot of it you will probably later reject, but usually the basis for your essay can be developed out of this material.

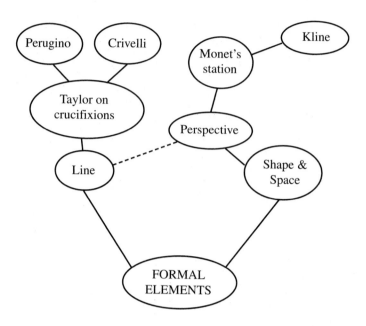

The following is an example of a prewriting exercise composed by a group of students in a class on Art Since 1940. As a way to generate more substantive discussion in class, I often divide the class into working groups of six or seven to pursue a given topic or problem together. One of their number agrees to take notes on the discussion, type them up, and then disseminate them to the group as an e-mail discussion group. Then, over a weekend, for instance, the group further refines their thinking. (I sometimes contribute to these discussions myself by asking questions set off in brackets.) In this case, the group was asked to consider the significance of the Hirshhorn Museum's decision to install, in 2003, the large sculpture *Brushstroke*, by Roy Lichtenstein, in the plaza in front of the museum facing the National Mall in Washington, DC (Figure 35). Given the Hirshhorn's mission, to serve as the Smithsonian Institution's venue for international modern and contemporary art, what does this dramatic placement of Lichtenstein's sculpture tell us about how the museum understands the history of modern and contemporary art?

```
        What does it mean to put a huge work of Pop art
    in front a museum, in front of THE national museum
    of modern and contemporary art? Pop is what?
    anti-High Art, a celebration of popular culture, a
    condemnation of popular culture (both?), an explic-
    it attack on abstract expressionist painting—yes!
    hence the brushstroke, which, for abstract expres-
```

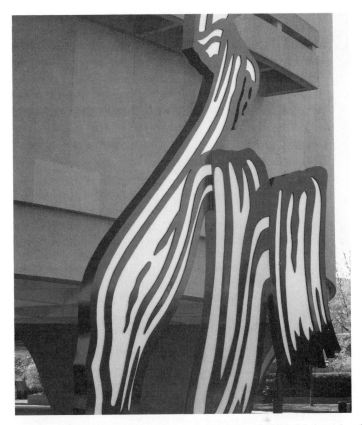

Figure 35   Roy Lichtenstein, *Brushstroke*, model completed 1996, fabricated and installed 2003. Painted and fabricated aluminum, 32 ft. 3 in. × 21 ft. × 6 ft. Hirshhorn Museum and Sculpture Garden, Smithsonian Institution, Washington, D.C., Joseph H. Hirshhorn Purchase Fund, 2002. Photo credit: Lee Stalsworth. © Estate of Roy Lichtenstein.

sionists embodied feeling, authentic feeling. Now it's emptied of feeling—it's a cartoon! Remember, Lichtenstein painted using the Ben Day dots that are used to print color in the newspaper's Sunday comics! Also remember what Warhol said about the Abstract Expressionists, how different their world was from Pop's: "The art world sure was different in those days. I tried to imagine myself in a bar striding over to, say, Roy Lichtenstein and asking him to 'step outside' because I'd heard he had insulted my soup cans. I mean, how corny. I was glad those slug-it-out routines had been retired—they weren't my style, let alone my capability."[1] So this is to suggest that Pop's "style" is something

totally different than the macho abstract expressionist approach? Yes, it suggests less personal
investment in the image—remember Warhol called his
studio The Factory, and wanted the work to look
like it was mechanically reproduced. Like a frame
in the Sunday comics? Exactly! So the *Brushstroke*
sculpture is an indictment of abstract expressionist "feeling," and it harks back to brushstroke
paintings that Lichtenstein did in the early
sixties [see Figure 36].

Hold it. Are we suggesting then that the Hirshhorn, by putting this sculpture in front of the museum, is attacking the abstract expressionists? No,
of course not. Its collection is built on abstract
expressionist work. So by putting the *Brushstroke*
out in front it isn't claiming to be anti-High Art
or pro-Pop Art, it's just putting the two in dialogue. Sure, look at the building that the sculpture sits in front of. It's High Modernism if you

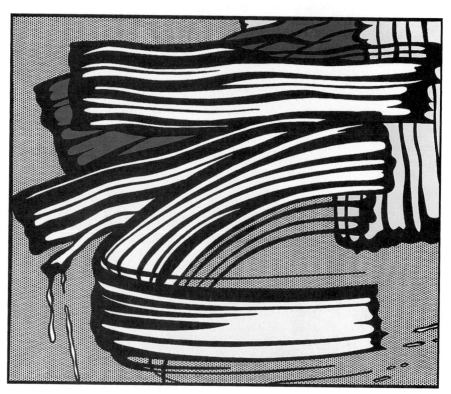

Figure 36   Roy Lichtenstein, *Little Big Painting*, 1964. Oil and synthetic polymer on
canvas, 68 × 80 in. Collection of the Whitney Museum of American Art, New York.
© Estate of Roy Lichtenstein.

ever saw it. Who's the architect? Gordon Bunshaft, of the New York firm Skidmore, Owings, and Merrill, responsible for a lot of Mies van der Rohe–like glass and steel buildings in the fifties and then, later, curved concrete structures like the Hirshhorn, which in its round drum shape echoes and pays homage to Frank Lloyd Wright's Guggenheim in NYC.... Even better, it contrasts dramatically with the sculpture on the other side of the Hirshhorn, Alexander Calder's *Two Discs* [see Figure 37]. I mean, talk about a Modernist icon! Its abstraction is the very opposite of Lichtenstein's realism. But Lichtenstein's *Brushstroke* doesn't represent anything. It represents a brushstroke. Yeah, but an abstract brushstroke. So you're on to something— that Lichtenstein's *Brushstroke* opens up a dialogue on the nature of abstraction. Yeah, in its giant scale it parodies the monumentality of a Jackson Pollock canvas. But, on the other hand, you could

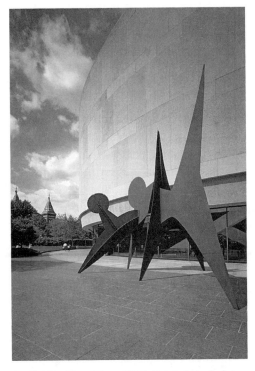

Figure 37   Alexander Calder, *Two Discs*, 1965. Painted steel plate and bolts, 25 ft. 6 in. × 27 ft. 4 in. × 17 ft. 4 in. Hirshhorn Museum and Sculpture Garden, Smithsonian Institution, Washington D.C. Gift of Joseph H. Hirshhorn, 1966. Photograph by Ricardo Blanc. © 2005 Estate of Alexander Calder/Artists Rights Society (ARS), New York.

say it parodies American advertising—the billboard.
I think you have to say both—pop culture and high
culture.
    We're forgetting something else that's really
important—the fact that it's a sculpture that
represents paint. Isn't that a little weird? I
mean, when he painted a brushstroke that was one
thing, but to sculpt a brushstroke, that's another.
He's transforming not only its scale, but its medium. So the piece in some sense symbolizes transformation? Is that it? I guess. What better message to
convey on the outside of a museum? Or maybe it
speaks to the way that art always grows out of
other art? The way that the arts cross-fertilize
each other. How about the way that the arts transform one another? The way that something like the
brushstroke, once full of personal feeling and
emotion, can be transformed into something ironic,
comic, is like the way that paint is transformed
into sculpture, a tiny brushstroke into a giant
piece of signage. And how about this?—the private
mark into the focus, there on the Mall, of social
space?

This exercise is full of good ideas, and these students went on, from this beginning, to write their own essays. But one of the most important things for you to recognize in this example is that the group quickly resorted to comparative methods in order to address Lichtenstein's work, comparing it not only to Lichtenstein's earlier brushstroke paintings, but also to abstract expressionist painting and modernist sculpture and architecture. As we discussed in Chapter 1, comparative essays have the advantage of explaining change, in this case both the formal and art historical transformations that Lichtenstein's sculptural *Brushstroke* embodies.

Online Writing
    More and more, students are engaged in the kind of writing that is represented by the preceding example—that is, they write in **e-mail, list-serve, chat room, newsgroup,** or **blog** environments. Today, many publishers are creating Web sites for their textbooks, and included in these sites are discussion environments, or chat rooms, where students from around the country can engage one another on issues raised by the text. Many online services also organize chat rooms. In addition, as the example above demonstrates, instructors are increasingly requiring students to participate in local e-mail discussion groups. These are generally designed

to serve two purposes: first, they provide the student with an opportunity to write on a routine basis; and second, they provide a forum in which students can share information and debate issues. Instructors often oversee these groups, both to monitor your progress as a writer (and thinker) and to get a sense of what their class is thinking about. Finally, students are increasingly organizing discussion groups on their own.

Many students find the e-mail environment to be liberating. Where they are loathe to speak up in class, they feel more comfortable behind the screen of their computer. There are no time constraints, no pressure. They can think about what they want to say, and say exactly what they mean. Furthermore, e-mail is probably the least formal of the writing media. E-mail communication is not exactly talking, but it often seems far closer to talking than to writing. It is perhaps best thought of as written conversation. As a result, most e-mail writing is relatively short. No one enjoys scrolling down a long e-mail message any more than they enjoy listening to someone dominate a class discussion.

What kinds of discussion and writing are appropriate for the e-mail environment? Most students find that the most common form of communication is the question and answer format. If you are researching a particular topic, you might briefly describe what you are doing and ask if anyone has found any interesting related sources (or who checked out a particular book from the library, and can you see it too). Or you might question a student's sources. I have elided, in the discussion above, an interchange about how the student knew that the architect of the Hirshhorn was Gordon Bunshaft. The answer: "I looked up the Hirshhorn's home page." But don't ask a question that you could answer yourself with a little effort. Don't ask if anyone knows Lichtenstein's birth date, or the size of the height of the *Brushstroke* sculpture. But you can test an argument: "I'm beginning to think that one way to approach this topic is to see the *Brushstroke* not so much as a parody of abstract expressionism as an homage to it." The response to this suggestion was interesting. Some pointed out that originally, in the sixties, Lichtenstein had clearly intended the brushstroke to be parodic, and therefore it probably remained so. Others pointed out that in the forty years or so since Lichtenstein had originally painted the brushstroke, certain aspects of abstract expressionism had come to be seen as anticipating Pop art itself. In the words of Allan Kaprow, the originator of the Happening, " Pollock . . . left us at the point where we must become preoccupied with and even dazzled by the space and objects of our everyday life"—objects like the Sunday comics.[2] This debate initiated a fruitful discussion. If you think of your group as a sounding board, and if you treat the others with the same respect that you think you deserve, the group can function as if it were an online seminar, going on all the time outside the classroom.

There are a number of pitfalls that you need to be aware of if you are writing in an e-mail environment. It is advisable, if you choose to participate in a discussion group that is open to the entire Web-linked community, to "lurk" for a few days, observing the level of the conversation and the behavior of the participants. You might find yourself in what amounts to an ongoing scholarly research conference, and as a result you may want to "lurk" forever—learning but not participating. Or you might find yourself in a group that likes to "flame" newcomers—that is, treat them with abusive remarks. Another question that arises in the online environment is the matter of intellectual property. In an ideal world, everyone would give you the credit you deserve for your ideas, but not everyone will. If you put forth an idea in an open e-mail environment, expect to see someone else use it, and without acknowledging you. Yet another problem is stylistic. Some e-mail systems currently have no mechanism to indicate italics, boldface, underlining, and so on, though, increasingly, they can accommodate accent marks. When you cite e-mail sources in your own work, you need to be careful to add these back in—you will need to italicize titles, for instance. Also, we are not all equally proficient as writers. This means that we need to respect the efforts of those less able than ourselves, and it also means that not everyone is able to communicate exactly what they mean. Don't hurry to take offense in an online environment. Be patient. Finally, remember that electronic conversations have a kind of permanence that real-time conversations lack. You go on record on e-mail—messages are generally archived for long periods of time, even if they disappear off your screen. If you say something you should not, you may regret it. Be careful about what you say in e-mail, and be careful how you say it.

CREATING A FINISHED ESSAY

Organizing Your Essay: From Description to the Verbal Frame

One of my favorite exercises in teaching a writing-intensive course for studio art majors is to have my students write about Sean Scully's 2002 painting *Vincent* (see the front cover). I tell them nothing about it. I simply project the image in class and ask them to write about it for ten minutes. Here are three examples:

```
Compositionally, this painting is set up with blocks
of color pushing and pulling with each other. By
stacking the blocks, Scully creates a loose grid.
```

Beneath the grid, hints of the underpainting show
through, lending a sense of depth to an otherwise
flat composition.

The edges of Scully's rectangular blocks vi-
brate. Behind the orchres and greens, a red shows
through, more vibrant and primary than any of the
other colors. It is as if light shines through and
escapes form the sides of the darker rectangles. As
a result, the shapes seem almost organic rather
than geometric, pushing against one another as if
alive.

Sean Scully is a master of joining edges. Every
edge is intentionally dynamic, his underpainting
showing through. The painterly quality of his
brushwork seems at odds with the geometric regularity of his composition. Although his blocks are
slightly different sizes, they are, with a single
exception, grouped in pairs that evoke the balance
of the square. At the bottom right, however, three
blocks are stacked into a tall rectangle. It is as
if Scully wants to approach regularity and orderli-
ness, even as he fights against it. It is interesting that Scully named the painting *Vincent*. Perhaps
it is about van Gogh's own spiritual struggle—his
desire for balance, and his inability to ever quite
find it.

The class then shared their responses, and they agreed that the key
concepts articulated by the group included the importance of the edge to
Scully's work, the sense of dynamism, vibrancy, and liveliness achieved
through the appearance of the red underpainting, the push and pull of the
grid, and the tension between the geometry of the grid and his sensuous
brushwork. The class was uniformly interested in the connection made in
the last example to the work of Vincent van Gogh.

In other words, in confronting the painting's title, the class stepped
into the necessity of confronting the painting's verbal frame. Understanding this necessity is, in fact, the point of the exercise: Formal description
can take them only so far. I ask them all, then, to research the painting and
come back with their findings the following week. I do not, at this point
in the term, ask for a formal essay, because the real point is for them to get
acquainted with the library and the resources available to them on the Internet. But their findings are instructive.

They learned, in the first place, that Scully's painting is indeed an
homage to Vincent van Gogh, and specifically to his 1888 painting,
Vincent's Chair with Pipe (see the back cover). In the catalogue to

Scully's 2005 exhibition, *Wall of Light*, which traveled widely across the United States, van Gogh's painting is reproduced alongside Scully's. In the accompanying essay, written by curator Stephen Bennett Phillips, the students learned that when he was seventeen, he discovered van Gogh's painting in the Tate Museum in London (it is now in the National Gallery) and was particularly attracted to "the architecture of the painting . . . [and] the light and shadow captured on the planes of the chair."[3] Van Gogh's brushwork, espeicially in the block-like tiles of the floor, also appealed to him. The coloration of Scully's painting is, of course, inspired by the color of van Gogh's floor. But Scully was also moved by van Gogh's spiritual idealism. In a bookstore he discovered an edition of van Gogh's letters, which he stole. As Phillips affirms in his essay, Scully still has the book, "and it continues to guide him."[4]

Several students were curious about what van Gogh had to say about his chair in his letters. There they found, in Letter 571, written to his brother Theo on November 23, 1888, this explanation of his technique in the painting: "I have tried for an effect of light by means of clear color," he wrote.[5] Van Gogh's statement resonates deeply with the title of Scully's exhibition, *Wall of Light*—both artists evidently seek to reveal light. But it is not the radiant light of hope. Rather, as Michael Auping has put it in his own catalogue essay to the *Wall of Light* exhibition, "When Scully speaks of light, he is also talking about its twin opposite." Auping continues: "Scully's light is somber. While many artists seek to bring light out of dark, Scully seems intent on bringing darkness to light, as if he were revealing a deeper inner secret."[6] What he shares most deeply with van Gogh is the psychological complexity of his light, and the way, as one student put it, his walls of light "both defy and represent logic and stability."

It is easy to understand that what the students had begun to develop here was a very interesting comparative essay. They quickly came to understand what is at stake in Scully's painting by comparing it to van Gogh's. Because comparative essays are so useful in analyzing works of art, they are probably the favorite form of essay question posed in art history exams. It is crucial, therefore, for you to decide how you want to approach the problem of writing them. In my course on nineteenth-century European Art, I have occasionally asked students to compare the Spanish artist Francisco Goya's portrait of the *Countess of Chinchón* (Figure 38) to the French painter Jacques Louis David's portrait of *Madame Trudaine* (Figure 39) by considering how each reflected the artist's sense of life in early nineteenth-century Europe. One particularly good essay began like this: "Working at essentially the same time, under the shadow of the French Revolution and the social chaos it instigated, David and Goya arrived at radically different

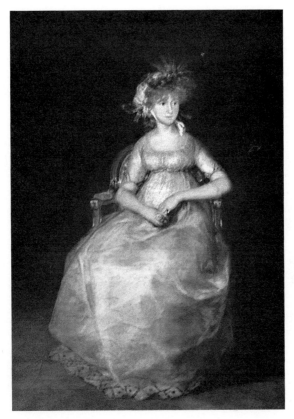

Figure 38   Francisco Goya, *Countess of Chinchón*, 1800. Oil on canvas,
85 in. × 56¾ in. Duque de Sueca Collection, Madrid. © AFP/CORBIS

styles. But both responded, in their individual ways, to the turmoil and confusion of their age." Then the writer analyzed David's painting: "David attempts to control his world, imposing linear order upon it," and so on.
Finishing that analysis, she turned to Goya: "The order David achieves is
abandoned by Goya," the second half of the essay begins. But throughout
the second half, she continually refers back to her analysis of the David.
"Whereas David subjects his world to a rigid grid that controls space, Goya
buries all his world in an atmosphere of shade and darkness, which causes
us to lose our bearings and become lost in his space." Her conclusion begins: "It is as if Goya reveals what is buried in David, opens his imagina-
tion to the terror and doubt that David controls with mathematical
precision. But both recognize the terrible insecurity of the times. Goya is
willing to admit his compassionate feeling for his sitter, while David in-
spires his to discover her own strength and courage."

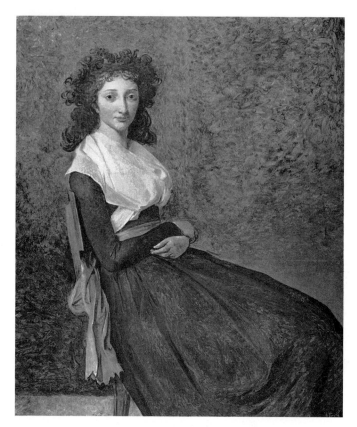

Figure 39 Jacques Louis David, *Madame Charles Louis Trudaine, born Micault de Courbetan* (1769–1802), sometimes known as *Madame Chalgrin*, 1791. Oil on canvas, 4 ft. 3¼ in. × 3 ft. 2½ in. Musée du Louvre, Paris. Courtesy the Réunion des musées nationaux.

I recommend that you try to write comparative essays by using this model. Begin by stating in general terms what it is that the comparison between X and Y reveals. Analyze one of the two works in question rather fully. Then analyze the second, always remembering to compare and contrast it to the first. A second approach is probably more common:

I. General Introduction of the two works (X & Y)
II. First point of comparison (e.g., subject matter)
    A. Similarities between X & Y
    B. Differences between X & Y
III.Second point of comparison (e.g., space)
    A. Similarities between X & Y
    B. Differences between X & Y . . . . and so on.

The difficulty with this approach is that it's like watching tennis: Back and forth you go, left and right, X and Y, X and Y, X and Y. . . . I don't recommend it.

But whichever model you choose, remember this: The object is not to list the similarities and differences between two works for the sake of listing them, but, rather, to reveal, through the comparison, important features and traits of the works that would otherwise be lost or obscure. More to the point, the comparison must have a focus. Your essay must have a thesis.

Developing an Argument or Thesis

A formal analysis of a work of art can be distinguished from its formal description by virtue of the fact that it takes into account the *meaning* of the formal elements it describes. It asks not only *what* the artists have accomplished in formal terms but *why* they have made the decisions they have. In other words, the function of the preliminary writing exercises suggested in the preceding pages is to help you discover ideas about the significance of the subject matter (the particular work or works of art) you have chosen to write about. They are designed to help you discover an argument or *thesis*. For instance, Pollock's *Full Fathom Five* might be your subject matter, but your thesis consists of the central idea or point you wish to make about the painting. If you were to write a short paper on *Full Fathom Five*, you might state your thesis in terms such as this: "While, at first glance, Pollock's painting seems to be little more than a random web of lines representing nothing, it can be approached more productively as an investigation of the possibilities of representation itself." Such a thesis statement marks the difference between the kind of writing samples presented so far and the next example, which was built out of the group prewriting exercise on Lichtenstein's *Brushstroke*. Early in this text I said that all art involves conscious decisions, and I suggested that one way for you to recognize these decisions is to imagine other possible handlings of the particular work you are examining. Good comparative essays offer the most appropriate format in which you can recognize this kind of difference, which is after all a difference in intention and meaning. The real point of this final essay—its thesis—is that although both versions of Lichtenstein's brushstroke—painting and sculpture—begin from the same starting point, they reflect formal decisions that make for very different effects and result in very different meanings. The final draft of the essay concludes as follows (the notes can be found in the Notes section at the conclusion of this book):

> In the press release announcing the Hirshhorn's installation of Lichtenstein's sculpture on the plaza facing the Mall in 2003, the museum's director, Ned

Rifkin, proudly predicted that the *Brushstroke* was "sure to become an icon for visitors to our nation's capital"—something more, in other words, than just an image; something venerated, almost sacred.[7] Pop Art had long since understood its iconic status. Warhol's soup cans and Coca-Cola bottles had served as icons of America's worship of consumer goods, and his Marilyn Monroes and Elvis Presleys as iconic symbols of the nation's cult of personality. Yet for all their popular appeal, these icons were understood to be all show, no substance. "If you want to know about Andy Warhol," Andy once explained, "just look at the surface of my paintings and films and me, and there I am. There's nothing behind it."[8] The Pop icon was a symbol of expression emptied of feeling and devoid of meaning, and in this it was just like Lichtenstein's brushstroke paintings.

But in the brushstroke's transformation from painting to sculpture, across the forty-year gulf that lies between the brushstroke as enlarged comic strip image and the brushstroke as monumental representation of paint in steel, it somehow accumulated feeling and meaning. It came to represent the history of art, or at least the history of modern and contemporary art. Placed in the plaza in front of a museum, it assumed most of the attributes of the work it purportedly parodied, Jackson Pollock's drips and splashes, the surface skeins of paint that in paintings like *Guardians of the Secret or Full Fathom Five* seem to hide, just out of view, something "rich and strange" beneath. It speaks to the space that lies behind it, that lies unseen, inside the museum, to the mysteries of modern and contemporary art housed there. And in this, finally, it echoes Pollock's own famous summary of his own work:

energy and motion
made visible—
memories arrested in space[9]

Following on the heels of a well-developed argument outlining the transition, in the early 1960s, from the formal and painterly concerns of the abstract expressionists to the more social orientation of Pop art, this conclusion seem to bring these two apparently opposing tendencies in twentieth-century art together without doing any injustice to their distinct and unique features. But this conclusion, as strong as it is, was not a product of the writer's first, or even second draft. It was the product of an ongoing process of critical thinking and *revision*, first as it was shared with other students online, and then, later, after it was shared with me and revised for inclusion in this volume.

Revising and Editing

One of the great advantages of employing any of the ways to discover ideas for writing suggested in this chapter is that they will get you in the habit of writing multiple drafts of a paper. As you move from the prewriting stage to a more formal version of your argument, you will see your ideas develop and change. You will write an even better paper, however, if you set aside your first draft of the final version and return to it later, intent on revising your thinking once again. If you have the time, it is generally worth your while to revise your essay several times.

Revision demands that you be self-critical. It is different from editing, which is the last stage of the writing process. When you edit your final draft, you check for spelling mistakes, typos, proper punctuation, and so on. (Be sure, for instance, that names of works of art are italicized or underlined.) Do not rely on a simple spell check program provided in your software. A spell check will miss "there" when you mean "their," or "from" when you mean "form." Neither do you necessarily need to follow the advice that your software will give you under its grammar check program, but consider what it suggests. The simple fact is, no software yet can read your writing in context, and therefore it may not necessarily make proper decisions about your writing.

If you edit your paper on screen, remember that the screen literally blinds you to errors. When you print your paper, you will want to read it again. During revision, read the paper out loud. Doing this slows down the reading process, requires you to pay more attention than you otherwise might, and often reveals awkwardnesses that you can ignore when reading silently. It also allows you to "hear" whether your ideas hold together. You need to recognize at what point your argument is weaker than it should be, where you fail to state your case as strongly as you might, when you've chosen a word that is too general or too vague. Also you need to take time to make corrections.

On the following two pages is a set of questions that is particularly appropriate for writing about art. We've placed them on a separate spread, by themselves, in order to allow you to photocopy the spread and check off each question to which you believe you can answer "yes." You will be tempted to answer "yes" to all of these questions when you really mean "more or less." Don't let yourself get away with this. Not until you can answer "yes" in all honesty—when, that is, you are being honestly self-critical—will your paper finally be ready to hand in. Following this check-list is an example of what your final essay might look like if indeed you can answer yes to all the questions. It is a model essay, the final product of an act of critical thinking that is the process of writing about art.

A Revision Checklist

The Essay as a Whole

__1 Have you clearly stated and developed your thesis?

__2 Have you focused on particular works of art in order to support your thesis?

__3 Have you discussed these works of art in sufficient detail?

__4 Have you adequately considered the significance or meaning of the works, as opposed to merely describing them?

__5 Have you satisfactorily accounted for the title(s) of the work(s) of art you are discussing?

__6 Have you considered how these works reflect larger art historical issues and tendencies?

__7 Is your argument logical? Does it make sense?

Paragraphs

__1 Does your introduction clearly state your thesis?

__2 Are connections between paragraphs clear? Does one follow logical-ly from the other?

__3 Does your conclusion provide a satisfying sense of completion?

__4 Are your paragraphs well developed? Does each contain concrete, specific examples in support of a general idea? Are these examples interesting and persuasive?

__5 Have you quoted primary and secondary sources effectively?

__6 Does quoted material further your own argument?

__7 Have you avoided relying too heavily on outside sources?

__8 Have you avoided concluding your paragraphs with quotations? (If not, this is a good indication that you are relying on others and not developing an argument of your own.)

Sentences and Words

__1 Are facts, figures, and dates accurate?

__2 Are footnotes accurate?

___3 Have you footnoted all the material and ideas that you found in primary and secondary sources?

___4 Are there consistently no more than two or three footnotes per typed page? (If there are more, this is another indication that you are relying too much on the thinking of others and not enough on your own ideas.)

___5 Have you used exact words? Is your vocabulary describing formal elements, principles of design, and media and materials accurate?

___6 Is your language concrete and specific rather than general and vague?

___7 Is your choice of words properly formal? (You probably want to avoid slang and jargon.)

___8 Have you avoided sexist language?

___9 Have you avoided clichés?

WRITING ABOUT ART: THE FINAL PRODUCT

The following essay, by Sharon Lautenschlager, a student in a nineteenth-century painting survey, expands upon its discussion of a particular painting—David's *Portrait of Madame Trudaine* (Figure 39)—just enough to make it resonate not only with David's other work of the period, but with the circumstances surrounding the French Revolution as a whole. The painting becomes as much a portrait of the Revolution itself as of a particular French woman. In fact, an interesting problem was encountered in the course of researching this paper in preparation for publication here: The painting is referred to in the scholarship sometimes as a portrait of *Madame Trudaine*, but more often as a portrait of one *Madame Chalgrin*. According to the Louvre, however, the painting is now believed to be a portrait of Madame Charles Louis Trudaine, born Micault de Courbeton in 1769 and who died in 1802. The only way I can account for this discrepancy is to suggest that, in the confusion of the Revolution, even the identity of David's sitter was lost for a time. Lautenschlager's essay seems to capture this spirit of contradiction and discrepancy. No great amount of learning was required for her to write it, and yet the paper seems convincing, even learned. It is an example of words and images coming together in a way that enriches them both. This is admittedly a very good paper. It has, furthermore, undergone several revisions, the last with considerable input from me in preparation for publication here, so that I could provide you, in the end, with a "model" essay. But it remains, by and large, Lautenschlager's work, and it represents an example of writing about art that is not, I submit, beyond your reach.

Painting the Revolution:
David's *Portrait of Madame Trudaine*
Sharon Lautenschlager

The opening sentence of Charles Dickens's *Tale of Two Cities* speaks eloquently of the essential contradictions and conflicts of the French Revolution: "It was the best of times, it was the worst of times, it was the age of wisdom, it was the age of foolishness... it was the season of Light, it was the season of Darkness, it was the spring of hope, it was the winter of despair. . . ." The *Portrait of Madame Trudaine*, painted by Jacques Louis David in 1790-91, speaks as eloquently in visual terms of these same conflicts. This portrait is at the same time rigidly geometric and wildly passionate; it simultaneously pulls you in and pushes back at you; it is both coldly mathematical and warmly human. The composition is almost aggressively simple, and yet every element has been carefully contrived to create a specific kind of effect. Anita Brookner has said in her study of David that "David did not influence the Revolution; the Revolution influenced David."[1] His *Portrait of Madame Trudaine* bears witness to that influence.

Everything in this picture argues against something else; but everything in the picture also repeats and confirms something else. The disturbing, unsettling impact is first created by two devices, and close examination reveals multitudes of other devices that serve to maintain and enhance the original impact. One of the major "contradictions" is the color. David has painted this portrait with two sets of nearly complementary colors—dark orange and green for the larger color masses, and less intense blue and yellow for the two smaller areas. These two pairs of opposites, plus white, comprise the total palette of the picture. The second, equally important contradiction is the contrast between the absolute stillness of the sitter's posture and expression, and the wild freedom of the brushstroke throughout most of the picture, a quality that cannot be dismissed as merely a function of the painting's possibly "unfinished" state since this same brushwork appears throughout David's work in technically "finished" paintings.[2]

The painting can be broken up into almost endless geometric balances and repetitions, parallels

and perpendiculars, diagonals that divide, angles
that repeat one another, and ovals and curves that
appear over and over again. For example, diagonals
drawn from each upper corner to each opposing lower
corner would intersect at the hands, which are thus
precisely centered top-to-bottom and side-to-side.
The right half of the painting consists of two
shapes, the background and the skirt of the sitter's dress, both of which are painted without dimension or detail, and both of which echo each
other's shape. Another pair of shapes, on the left
side of the painting, echo each other exactly in
shape and dimension, but oppose one another in
color and direction—these are the small yellow
rectangle of the floor and the large orange rectangle formed by a subtle but unmistakable value shift
in the otherwise random "scumbling" of the background, which makes a vertical line running from
the top of the canvas to the sitter's hands. This
barely perceptible line runs parallel to the sides
of the frame, as does another implied line, formed
by the sitter's nose, chin, the shadow line on the
throat, the elbow, the sash, and finally the leg of
the chair. The sash of the woman's dress has been
strategically arranged to break up what would have
been the curve of the back of the chair—a curve
that could not have worked in the composition. A
graceful or seductive tilt to the head would have
been equally out of place here, so Madame Trudaine
holds herself rigidly erect, with her face turned
at an uncomfortably sharp angle to the body, with
the eyes and mouth on a plane exactly parallel to
the top and bottom of the frame, as well as the
floor line. What cannot be made horizontal or
vertical in the composition are curves in the face
and hands, but these are made to repeat themselves.
The oval of the face is the same oval as the left
hand, and the same again as the eyes. The sharp
curve of the end of the nose is the same curve as
the end of the chin, and this angle is repeated in
the crook of the arm and the end of the sash. The
triangle between the chair leg and dress is repeated by shapes on the torso. This playing with line
and shape could go on indefinitely.

Opposing this rigidly ordered geometry is the
human element of the portrait. There is a very appealing frankness and openness in the expression of
Madame Trudaine, which is confirmed by the graceful
curve of the visible hand and the enigmatic smile.

While the unkempt hair and utter simplicity of the dress indicate a disarming absence of personal vanity, the sharply contrasted but modestly formed bodice indicates a gentle femininity that is very appealing. Balancing and opposing this warmth, however, is the rigidly upright and tightly self-contained pose that utterly denies any invitation to intimacy expressed in the face. Beyond the pose, the composition conspires to push the figure out aggressively at the viewer by the absence of any perspectival depth. Not only has architectural detail been eliminated (no corners, window, shadows of any kind), but even the cropping, which eliminates any visible contact between the chair and sitter with the floor, prohibits orientation of Madame Trudaine in a logical space. With nothing but a geometric grid to hold her in place, the aggressive color of the background pushes her forward. While the woman's facial expression is warm and open, her body language is rigid and self-contained. While the composition is all order and simplicity, the brushwork and color are all freedom and extravagance. The effect is one of extreme tension, or of passion restrained.

David produced this painting during the first years of the Revolution, a year after *Brutus and the Lictors*, and two years before *Marat*. At the same time as this was painted, he was struggling to finish *The Tennis Court Oath*. In his monograph on David, Antoine Schnapper informs us that in the Versailles sketchbook David has scrawled a note to himself noting that the Trudaine brothers had subscribed for two prints each of the engraving of *The Tennis Court Oath*.[3] The younger brother, Charles Michel, had commissioned *The Death of Socrates*, and the elder, Charles Louis, had just commissioned David's portrait of his wife. The brothers were among David's most devoted and interested patrons, and discussions with the two and their circle of friends had evidently been profoundly influential upon David's conception of not only *The Death of Socrates* but also *The Oath of the Horatii*.[4] Nevertheless, as so often happened, on the eve of the 9th Thermidor, in July 1794, the two brothers were both guillotined.

The *Portrait of Madame Trudaine* is an intensely emotional painting, deeply involved in the passionate struggle to create a new order of things and yet deeply conscious of the need to submit these

passions to order and discipline. Her costume, as
Norman Bryson has put it, "is stridently republi-
can. . . . Her strained impassive expression and
the resignation of her folded arms indicate acceptance of the changing times; it is almost the atti-
tude of a person under arrest, a person awaiting
sentence."[5] Like *The Tennis Court Oath*, the *Portrait
of Madame Trudaine* is a painting literally undone
by history. If not actually left unfinished by its
subject's—and society's—fall from grace, then it
is painted so as to feel unfinished, undone, the
emblem of change itself.

Notes

1. Anita Brookner, *Jacques-Louis David* (New
York: Harper & Row, 1980), 82.

2. Jean Clay, in his *Romanticism* (New York:
Vendome Press, 1981), 121, notes the similarity of
this painting to David's *Portrait of Monsieur de
Joubert*, painted five years earlier, in 1786. I
have relied on the illustration in Clay's book for
my discussion of the painting's color.

3. Antoine Schnapper, *David*, trans. Helga Harrison (New York: Alpine Fine Arts, 1980), 129.

4. Brookner, 83.

5. Norman Bryson, *Tradition and Desire: From
David to Delacroix* (Cambridge, England: Cambridge
University Press, 1984), 161.

Appendix
A SHORT GUIDE
TO USAGE AND STYLE
The Rules and Principles
of Good Writing

QUICK REFERENCE

Possessive Apostrophes, p. 123
Commas, p. 123
Comma Splices, p. 124
Run-on Sentences, p. 125
That and *Which*, p. 125
Titles, p. 125
Foreign Phrases, p. 126
Split Infinitives, p. 126
Sentence Fragments, p. 127
Colons (:), p. 127
Semicolons (;), p. 127
Dashes, p. 128
Parentheses, p. 129
Quotations, p. 129
Ellipses (...), p. 130

Dangling Modifiers, p. 131
Subject-Verb Agreement, p. 131
Pronoun Agreement, p. 132
Pronouns and Gender Issues,
  p. 132
Indefinite Antecedents (*it* and *this*),
  p. 132
Correlative Expressions, p. 133
Verb Tense Consistency, p. 134
Diction Consistency, p. 134
Concrete and Specific Language,
  p. 135
Frequently Misspelled Words,
  p. 135

1. **Possessive Apostrophes** The possessive apostrophe is one of the most misused—and neglected—of all the elements of usage. Indicate the possessive singular of all nouns by adding an *'s*, no matter with what letter the noun ends:

Incorrect	*Correct*
the artists work	the artist's work
Wyndham Lewis' drawings	Wyndham Lewis's drawings
Juan Gris' painting	Juan Gris's painting

The possessive pronouns—*hers*, *yours*, *ours*, *its*, and *theirs*—do not employ the apostrophe. This is especially confusing in regard to *its*. *It's* is the contraction of "it is."

Incorrect	*Correct*
Consider it's form.	Consider its form.
Its important to think about form.	It's important to think about form.

Indicate the possessive plural of all nouns ending in *s* by placing an apostrophe after the concluding *s*. Plural nouns ending in letters other than *s*—such as *women* and *media*—employ an *'s*.

Incorrect	*Correct*
the artists club	the artists' club
the missionaries purpose	the missionaries' purpose
the womens' building	the women's building

2. **Commas** Outlined below are several rules governing comma usage that should be followed in most situations. Commas are frequently overused, and almost as frequently, underutilized. If a comma seems to interfere with reading ease—that is, if it seems to draw attention to itself—consider eliminating it. Often, commas may be eliminated simply by rewriting your sentence.

Acceptable	*Better*
Mondrian, in the painting, employs three colors.	Mondrian employs three colors in the painting.

If by failing to employ a comma, you create ambiguity, insert one.

What Was Written	*What Was Meant*
Frequently painted images are confusing.	Frequently, painted images are confusing.

For a series of three or more terms, use a comma after each term except the last. Do not use a comma to introduce the series.

Incorrect	*Correct*
Picasso used oil, pencil and charcoal in the painting.	Picasso used oil, pencil, and charcoal in the painting.
The sculptor had a taste for, steel, iron, and concrete.	The sculptor had a taste for steel, iron, and concrete.

Parenthetical phrases are generally set off by a comma. Place a comma both before and after the parenthetical phrase. If the parenthetical phrase is long and complex, it is often better to use alternative punctuation, such as dashes or parentheses, in order to avoid confusion (see section 11 below).

Incorrect	*Correct*
The photograph it is important to realize depicts the scene of a crime.	The photograph, it is important to realize, depicts the scene of a crime.
Goya's etchings which were not published until long after his death are terrifying indictments of war.	Goya's etchings, which were not published until long after his death, are terrifying indictments of war.
The owner of the painting the Marquis of Toledo, neglected it for years.	The owner of the painting, the Marquis of Toledo, neglected it for years.

Before a conjunction that connects one independent clause to another, place a comma. To recognize two independent clauses, consider if the subject of the second clause is different from the subject of the first. If the subject changes, employ a comma. Remember: A switch from a noun to a pronoun represents a change in subject.

Incorrect	*Correct*
Georgia O'Keeffe loved the Southwest and the region deeply influenced her work.	Georgia O'Keeffe loved the Southwest, and the region deeply influenced her work.
Georgia O'Keeffe loved the Southwest and she painted it often.	Georgia O'Keeffe loved the Southwest, and she painted it often.
O'Keeffe wandered continually through the New Mexico hills, and painted them often.	O'Keeffe wandered continually through the New Mexico hills and painted them often.

3. Comma Splices   Do not join together two independent clauses by means of a comma. Add a conjunction, create two separate sentences, or employ a semicolon. Use of the semicolon emphasizes the close connection between the two independent clauses (see section 11 on page 127).

Incorrect	*Correct*
Georgia O'Keeffe loved the Southwest, the region deeply influenced her work.	Georgia O'Keeffe loved the Southwest, and the region deeply influenced her work.
	or, Georgia O'Keeffe loved the Southwest. The region deeply influenced her work.
	or, Georgia O'Keeffe loved the Southwest; the region deeply influenced her work.

4. Run-on Sentences   Do not join together two complete sentences as if they were one.

Incorrect	*Correct*
The audience did not appreciate the painting they were blind to its beauty.	The audience did not appreciate the painting. They were blind to its beauty.

5. *That* and *Which*   These two pronouns are consistently misused, the latter appearing where the former should. In contemporary spoken usage, *which* seems to be supplanting *that*, and it sometimes can be difficult to follow the "rule" and use *that* when *which* sounds better. Nevertheless, the "rule" is a simple one: *that* introduces restrictive clauses, *which* non-restrictive clauses. A restrictive clause is one *that* limits or defines its reference. A nonrestrictive clause, on the other hand, is parenthetical. Thus, if you sense that commas should be employed in your sentence, *which* in this sentence is precisely the case, use *which*. But if you sense that the addition of a comma would disrupt the flow *that* your sentence demands, use *that* and no commas.

Incorrect	*Correct*
This is the painting which Leonardo painted in 1506.	This is the painting that Leonardo painted in 1506.

6. Titles   Titles of works of art, books, and journals are italicized. Titles of short works, such as individual poems and journal articles, are put in quotation marks. If available on your word processor, use italics. If you handwrite, on an exam for instance, or type, indicate italics by underlining the title (a single underline is the editorial mark used to signify italics). Also note below that the title of Frida Kahlo's painting *The Two Fridas* is shortened, after the possessive, to Kahlo's *Two Fridas*.

Incorrect	*Correct*
Michelangelo's David	Michelangelo's *David* (word processed) *or*, Michelangelo's David (handwritten or typed)
John Richardson's biography, A Life of Picasso	John Richardson's biography, *A Life of Picasso* (or, A Life of Picasso)
The article, Kahlo's Two Fridas, appeared in Art in America.	The article, "Kahlo's *Two Fridas*," appeared in *Art in America*. (Or, The article, "Kahlo's Two Fridas," appeared in Art in America.)

7. **Foreign Phrases**   While you might prefer to avoid foreign phrases in general writing, you cannot avoid them in writing about art, because a good deal of specialized vocabulary based on foreign words has developed to describe various artistic effects. Italicize (or underline) such foreign phrases. Notice in the third example below that, without italics, the meaning of the phrase is confusing.

Incorrect	*Correct*
Magritte's trompe l'oeil paintings look real.	Magritte's *trompe l'oeil* paintings look real.
The painting's haziness derives from sfumato.	The painting's haziness derives from *sfumato*.
By means of passage, Cézanne blends different planes together.	By means of *passage*, Cézanne blends different planes together.

8. **Split Infinitives**   Generally, do not place an adverb in the middle of an infinitive construction. Occasionally, however, especially in less formal writing, to do otherwise will sound overly formal, even awkward, and will disrupt the flow of your writing. In such instances, splitting the infinitive is at least acceptable—and probably preferable.

Incorrect	*Correct*
He wanted to systematically print the edition.	He wanted to print the edition systematically.

Acceptable	*Also Acceptable*
He could never really learn to appreciate abstract art.	He could never learn to really appreciate abstract art.

9. **Sentence Fragments**   Make sure that each of your sentences contains a subject and a verb. Make sure you do not mistake a verb form ending with *-ing* (a participle) for a verb. Make sure you have not used a period when a comma is the proper punctuation.

Incorrect	*Correct*
The sculpture of the horse balances on one leg. A perfect example of the Han dynasty's mastery of bronze casting.	The sculpture of the horse balances on one leg, a perfect example of the Han mastery of bronze casting.
The drapery falls in deep folds and hollows. Contributing to the sense of reality in the work.	The drapery falls in deep folds and hollows, contributing to the sense of reality in the work.

10. **Colons**   Use the colon to introduce lists, or other amplification, and quotations (for quotations, see section 14 on page 129). When the introductory material is a complete sentence, use a colon after it. However, when the introductory material is not a complete sentence, use no punctuation. Do not use the colon after a verb, as in the second and third incorrect examples below.

Incorrect	*Correct*
A good caption should include these six things, the name of the artist, the title of the work, the date of execution, the work's medium, its dimensions, and its present location.	A good caption should include these six things: the name of the artist, the title of the work, the date of execution, the work's medium, its dimensions, and its present location.
A good caption should also include: the name of the artist, the title, etc.	
Picasso's point is: War is hell.	Picasso's point is simple: War is hell.

11. **Semicolons**   Use the semicolon in lists that are relatively long or complicated and to coordinate parallel ideas expressed in independent clauses. To avoid confusion, use semicolons to separate elements of a list when those elements themselves contain commas.

Incorrect	*Correct*
He saw three things: first, the painting's line, which was expressive, second, its color, which was also expressive, and finally, its overall design, which was curiously classical.	He saw three things: first, the painting's line, which was expressive; second, its color, which was also expressive; and finally, its overall design, which was curiously classical.

The semicolon is also useful as a coordinating conjunction—that is, as a way to join parallel constructions. Think of the semicolon as the fulcrum of a pair of perfectly balanced independent clauses, and you will use it to great effect. Indeed, its use is often most appropriate in contexts that imply balance of one kind or another, when, for instance, in two independent clauses we find *early* in the first and *later* in the second, or *on the one hand* in the first and *on the other hand* in the second, *sometimes* and *at other times*. Consider these examples:

Incorrect	*Correct*
On the one hand, Goya was dependent upon the monarchy. On the other hand, he appears to have despised it.	On the one hand, Goya was dependent upon the monarchy; on the other, he appears to have despised it.
Early in his career, the photographer concentrated on rendering light. He later transformed this interest by using light as a means to reveal form.	Early in his career, the photographer concentrated solely on rendering light; later, he rendered light in order to reveal form.

12. **Dashes**   Use dashes to set off a parenthetical phrase that itself contains punctuation, especially commas; use the dash to introduce a phrase that repeats and emphasizes elements you have already used in a sentence; and use it to introduce constructions beginning with *that is*, *namely*, *i.e.*, and so on. There is no space on either side of a dash. On word processors, the proper dash to employ is the so-called em-dash (a typographer's term). Since it is usually a special character, check your software manual for its keyboard location. On a typewriter, the em-dash is indicated by typing two consecutive hyphens—as we have shown here—again leaving no space on either side of the hyphens.

Acceptable	*Better*
The dealer sensed the situation, that, for whatever reason, his client was not pleased, unhappy perhaps with the painter's manner, and so he hastened to facilitate their departure.The dealer sensed the situation—that, for whatever reason, his client was not pleased, unhappy perhaps with the painter's manner—and so he hastened to facilitate their departure.	The dealer sensed the situation—that, for whatever reason, his client was not pleased, unhappy perhaps with the painter's manner— and so he hastened to facilitate their departure.
The painting was subdued, yet daring, subdued in its color, but daring in its scale.The painting was subdued, yet daring—subdued in its color, but daring in its scale.	The painting was subdued, yet daring—subdued in its color, but daring in its scale.
He taught painting as a profession, that is, as a way of life.	He taught painting as a profession—that is, as a way of life.

13. Parentheses   The first example above could as easily be punctuated with parentheses as dashes: "The dealer sensed the situation (that, for whatever reason, his client was not pleased, unhappy perhaps with the painter's manner), and so he hastened to facilitate their departure." Notice that there is no punctuation before the parentheses (never, under any circumstances, place a comma before parentheses), though a comma is necessary after the parenthetical expression. (An entire sentence, or several sentences, can also be placed in parentheses. When you do this, the final punctuation, a period or question mark, goes inside the final parenthesis.)

14. Quotations   Generally, introduce any quotation that is a complete sentence or longer with a colon and enclose it in quotation marks. All punctuation falls within the quotation marks.

Incorrect

In his 1886 novel, *The Masterpiece*, Emile Zola provides a fictionalized account of how Impressionist painting was initially received, "It was one long-drawn-out explosion of laughter, rising in intensity to hysteria. As soon as they reached the doorway, he saw visitors' faces expand with anticipated mirth".

In the example above, the quotation should be introduced with a colon and the final period should be inside the quotation marks:

Correct

In his 1886 novel, *The Masterpiece*, Emile Zola provides a fictionalized account of how Impressionist painting was initially received: "It was one long-drawn-out explosion of laughter, rising in intensity to hysteria. As soon as they reached the doorway, he saw visitors' faces expand with anticipated mirth."

Quotations shorter than a sentence are enclosed in quotation marks, but are subject to your own punctuation. The above example might be shortened, for instance, by writing it as follows:

Correct

In his 1886 novel, *The Masterpiece*, Emile Zola describes the "long-drawn-out explosion of laughter" that greeted Impressionist painting—a "mirth" that rose eventually, he says, to "hysteria."

Notice, incidentally, that even though only a single word is quoted at the sentence's end, the period still goes inside the quotation marks. If you turn to page 13 of this book, you will notice that the actual passage quoted from Zola's novel is much longer. If your quotation is longer than forty words, or approximately four lines, or if its lineation is important, as in poetry or a play, differentiate the quotation from the text proper by beginning on a new line and indenting the entire quotation five spaces. Such typographical indentation is a sign of quotation, *and so do not also use quotation marks.*

15. Ellipses   Both the quotations on pages 13 and 14 also make use of ellipses, or "dots" that indicate that material has been omitted from the original text. An ellipsis consists of three "dots," with a space before, after, and between each dot. When you are eliminating material from the middle of a sentence, use these three dots. When you eliminate a whole sentence or more, conclude the sentence before the ellipsis with a period, and then type the ellipsis as you normally would.

Original Quotation

The outside world must not come in, so windows are usually sealed off. Walls are painted white. The wooden floor is polished so that you click along clinically or carpeted so that you pad soundlessly, resting the feet while the eyes have at the wall. The art is free, as the saying used to go, "to take on its own life."

Brief of Part of One Sentence

The outside world must not come in, so windows are usually sealed off. Walls are painted white. The wooden floor is ... carpeted so that you pad soundlessly, resting the feet while the eyes have at the wall. The art is free, as the saying used to go, "to take on its own life."

Ellipsis of a Sentence or More

The outside world must not come in.... The art is free, as the saying used to go, "to take on its own life."

The last example above is so short—less than forty words and fewer than four lines—that it would not, if quoted, ever be indented. It would be enclosed in quotation marks. This would result, incidentally, in a quotation within a quotation. Use single quotation marks to indicate quotations within quotations.

Incorrect	*Correct*
"The outside world must not come in.... The art is free, as the saying used to go "to take on its own life."	"The outside world must not come in.... The art is free, as the saying used to go, 'to take on its own life.'"

16. **Dangling Modifiers**   Participial phrases at the beginning of sentences must refer to the subject of the sentence.

Incorrect	*Correct*
Being depressed, the painting seemed darker than it actually was.	Because I was depressed, the painting seemed darker than it actually was.

17. **Subject-Verb Agreement**   Make sure that your verb form is singular if the subject of your sentence is singular and plural if the subject of your sentence is plural. Do not be led astray by intervening words.

Incorrect	*Correct*
The use of paint, turpentine, and sand serve to create a unique surface.	The use of paint, turpentine, and sand serves to create a unique surface.
The proof of the pudding—the most telltale signs of the painter's genius and the hall-marks of her personal style—is wholly absent.	The proof of the pudding—the most telltale signs of the painter's genius and the hallmarks of her personal style—are wholly absent.

If sentences such as those on the right above sound awkward to your ear, consider rewriting them:

Correct	*Better*
The use of paint, turpentine, and sand serves to create a unique surface.	Paint, turpentine, and sand serve to create a unique surface.
The proof of the pudding—the most telltale signs of the painter's genius and the hall-marks of her personal style—is wholly absent.	The most telltale signs of the painter's genius and the hall-marks of her personal style—the proof of the pudding—are wholly absent.

Remember that when *none* means "not one" or "no one," it is singular and is used with a singular verb.

Incorrect	*Correct*
None of the paintings are finished.	None of the paintings is finished.

Remember that *each*, *every*, *either*, and *neither* also are singular and take singular verbs.

Incorrect	*Correct*
Each of the drawings are wonderful.	Each of the drawings is wonderful.
Every one of the sculptures were done in bronze.	Every one of the sculptures was done in bronze.
Neither of the portraits resemble him.	Neither of the portraits resembles him.

18. Pronoun Agreement   Make sure when you employ a plural pronoun that its referent is plural.

Incorrect	*Correct*
Each of the paintings must be judged on their own merits.	Each of the paintings must be judged on its own merits.
Neither of the students wanted to have their work subjected to criticism.	Neither of the students wanted to have his work subjected to criticism.

19. Pronouns and Gender Issues   When you employ a noun that is general in character—"the artist" or "the student," for instance—referring not to a specific artist or student but to the artist as a type or to the student body in general, pronoun reference to this antecedent is complicated by matters of gender. If I write, "The artist must always consider *his* medium," I have arbitrarily determined that the sex of "the artist" is male. Why not write, "The artist must always consider *his or her* medium"? Or, why not just, "The artist must always consider *her* medium"? Of course, choosing these last alternatives draws attention to your own awareness that there are subtle gender issues at play in our habits of usage. I recommend, however, that you avoid such constructions altogether by referring to such general types of people in the plural—by choosing for your noun "artists" instead of "the artist," or "students" instead of "the student." In this way, your prose will be gender neutral.

Acceptable	*Better*
If originality is what makes art great, then the artist must strive always to make his work original.	If originality is what makes art great, then artists must strive always to make their work original.
At this university, the student is allowed to realize his or her potential.	At this university, students are allowed to realize their potential.

20. Indefinite Antecedents   When you use the words *it* and *this*, be sure that their referents are clear to the reader. Very often writers expect these words to carry the complete sense of the sentence, or even paragraph, just completed. Generally, when you write the word *this* at the beginning of a sentence, always follow it with a noun or noun phrase—that is, do not leave its referent implied.

Ambiguous	*Clearer*
The viewer feels that there is humor in the work, but nowhere in the artist's writings does he say anything about it. [Does *it* refer to his humor or his work?]	The viewer feels that there is humor in the work, but nowhere in the artist's writings does he say anything about the painting.
The Chinese landscape painter works as a calligrapher might, emphasizing line to such a degree that his subject matter seems almost secondary, and yet the landscape is itself a gesture, endowed with meaning and feeling. This underscores the importance of calligraphy in Chinese art. [What does *this* refer to? The previous sentence, or a smaller fragment of it?]	The Chinese landscape painter works as a calligrapher might, emphasizing line to such a degree that his subject matter seems almost secondary, and yet the landscape is itself a gesture, endowed with meaning and feeling.

This emphasis on the gestural qualities to be found in nature itself underscores the importance of calligraphy in Chinese art. |

21. Correlative Expressions   Correlative expressions are phrases mutually related by terms such as *both/and*, and *not only/but also*. The phrases that follow such expressions should be parallel—that is, they should utilize the same grammatical construction.

Incorrect	*Correct*
Audubon's prints are both documentary in character and they possess their own formal beauty.	Audubon's prints possess both a documentary character and an inherent formal beauty.
Not only does he depict each specie accurately, but also each of his birds becomes an element in the design of the page.	He not only depicts each specie accurately but also incorporates each bird into the design of the page.

Incorrect	*Correct*
Audubon first approached his subjects in the wild, then he shot them, and finally they were stuffed so that he could study them in detail.	Audubon first approached his subjects in the wild, then shot them, and finally stuffed them so that he could study each specie in detail.

Notice that to correct each of the sentences above some rewriting was required. In the third example, for instance, the parallel structure of "shot them" and "stuffed them" made it awkward to repeat "study them" in the subordinate clause. The phrase was rewritten, therefore, to read "study each specie." Also pay close attention to the position of the subject in *not only/but also* constructions. If the subject occurs before the "not only," do not repeat it in the "but also" phrase. However, if the subject occurs after the "not only," then it must also be repeated after the "but also."

Incorrect	*Correct*
He not only paints, but he also sculpts.	He not only paints but also sculpts.
Not only has Nancy Holt worked in the desert but in urban environments.	Not only has Nancy Holt worked in the desert, but she has also created pieces in urban environments.

22. **Verb Tense Consistency** Never shift from one tense to another within a single sentence.

Incorrect	*Correct*
Caravaggio utilizes light in this work to new ends and, in so doing, created new emotional possibilities for painting.	Caravaggio utilizes light in this work to new ends and, in so doing, creates new emotional possibilities for painting.

Remember as well that when describing works of art in longer passages of a paragraph or even a few sentences in length, it is a convention of usage to employ the present tense throughout.

23. **Diction Consistency** Diction is word choice, and different kinds of writing call for different levels of diction. Writing can be informal in diaries or journals, for instance. But most written assignments call for more formal language. Generally, it is inappropriate to introduce colloquial or slang expressions into such formal writing.

Inappropriate	*Better*
The formalist critic does not believe in the possibility of a work of art being interesting on both aesthetic and political levels. Such a point of view is total baloney.	The formalist critic does not believe in the possibility of a work of art being interesting on both aesthetic and political levels. Such a point of view seems mistaken.

24. Concrete and Specific Language Good writing depends upon the richness of the detail it brings to bear upon a given subject. In writing about art, the more concrete and specific your descriptions, the better your writing will be. In coming up with concrete detail to describe general effects, you will almost certainly come to a better understanding of the work under discussion. The example in the left column below is part of an actual student response to an essay question on van Gogh's painting *The Night Café* (Figure 17). While there is nothing technically "wrong" with this answer, it is too vague to be interesting—or to receive a good grade. If its writer knows more, these sentences don't reveal it. It takes some effort to improve prose by making it more concrete, but you'll like your writing better, and probably receive a higher grade.

Too Vague	*Concrete and Specific*
Van Gogh's painting is unique. His use of color is highly dramatic, as is his application of paint. They combine to create a sense of tension that pervades the composition.	Van Gogh's painting is remarkable in its handling, in the way that his characteristic short and choppy brushstroke is laid against a broad, flat zone of color, a technique he usually reserved only for portraiture. The all-encompassing flatness of the red wall contrasts with the thickly painted rays of light emanating from the three lamps, with the awkward gestures that seem to sweep up the floor toward the door, and, most of all, with the deep green impasto of the billiard table. The tension created by the complementary contrast of red and green, meant by him to evoke the "terrible passions of humanity" present in the café, is thus underscored in the application of the paint itself.

25. Frequently Misspelled Words The following list is provided in order to alert you to those words that, in writing about art, I most frequently find misspelled. You would be wise to learn these.

affect ...not effect ("Affect" is a verb meaning to "influence"; "effect," when used as a verb, means to "bring about"; as a noun, it means "result.")

a lot ...not alot

all right ...not alright

chaos ...not kaos

color ...not colour (The second is the British spelling.)

column ...not colume

complementary color ...not complimentary

dimension ...not demension

effect ...not affect (See "affect" above.)

frieze ...not freeze

gray ...not grey (The second is the British spelling.)

illusion ...not allusion (Allusion means indirect reference.)

intaglio ...not intalio

light ...not lite

parallel ...not paralel

permanent ...not permenent or permanant

referring ...not refering

rhythm ...not rythm

separation ...not seperation

spatial ...not spacial (I've had as many as 50 of 55 students misspell this one on an exam.)

subtle ...not sutle

symbolic ...not symbollic

symmetry ...not symetry

there ...points to a place, as opposed to their, the plural possessive adjective, and they're, meaning "they are"

through ...not thru

too ...meaning "also" or "to an excessive degree" as in too cold, and spelled with two "o"s

twentieth-century art ...not twentieth century art (Used as an adjective such temporal designations employ a hyphen.)

volume ...not volumn (This word is often confused, apparently, with column.)

watercolor ...not water color

your professor's name ...No one notices if you spell it right, but to spell it wrong is to announce your inattention to detail.

NOTES

INTRODUCTION

1. Reprinted by permission of the publisher from THE PHILOSO-PHY OF ART by Arthur C. Danto, p. vi, Cambridge, Mass: Harvard University Press, Copyright © 1981 by Arthur C. Danto.

2. Arthur C. Danto, *After the End of Art: Contemporary Art and the Pale of History*, The A. W. Mellon Lectures in the Fine Arts, 1995 (Princeton, NJ: Princeton University Press, 1997), 4.

3. Ibid., xi–xii.

4. Ibid., xii.

5. Danto, Arthur C.; *After the End of Art*, © 1997 The Trustees of the National Gallery of Art, Washington DC/Published by Princeton Universtiy Press. Reprinted by permisison of Princeton University Press.

CHAPTER 1

1. Pierre Bourdieu and Alain Darbel, *L'Amour de l'Art* (Paris: Editions de Minuit, 1969), appendix 4, table 8.

2. Richard Serra, "*Tilted Arc* Destroyed," *Art in America* 77 (May 1989): 41.

3. Clara Weyergraf-Serra and Martha Busrick, eds., *The Destruction of* Tilted Arc*: Documents* (Cambridge, MA: MIT Press, 1991), 117.

4. Ibid., 67.

5. Brian O'Doherty, "Inside the White Cube: Notes on the Gallery Space," *Artforum* 14 (March 1976): 24–25.

6. Emile Zola, *The Masterpiece*, trans. Thomas Walton (Ann Arbor: University of Michigan Press, 1968), 128–29.

7. Milton W. Brown, *American Painting: From the Armory Show to the Depression* (Princeton, NJ: Princeton University Press, 1955), 113.

8. These arguments are more fully developed in my article, "American Vernacular: Objectivism, Precisionism, and the Aesthetics of the Machine," *Twentieth Century Literature* 35 (Fall 1989): 310–12.

9. Quoted in Douglas Crimp, "Richard Serra's Urban Sculpture: An Interview," in *Richard Serra: Interviews, Etc. 1970–1980* (Yonkers, NY: The Hudson River Museum, 1980), 170.

10. *Museum Without Walls*, André Malraux, © editions Gallimard, Paris, 1965. Translated by Stuart Gilbert and Francis Price, Secker & Warburg, 1967.

11. *The Internet as a Research Medium for Art Historians*, Leif Harmsen, April 1996. Http://www.harmsen.net/ahrc. Reprinted with permission of The Art History Research Center.

CHAPTER 2

1. Joshua Taylor, *Learning to Look: A Handbook for the Visual Arts* (Chicago: University of Chicago Press, 1957), 44, 50.

2. Ibid., 52.

3. Quoted in Katharine Kuh, *The Artist's Voice: Talks with Seventeen Artists* (New York: Harper & Row, 1962), 144.

4. Quoted in Irving Stone, *Dear Theo: The Autobiography of Vincent van Gogh* (New York: Doubleday, 1937), 383–84.

5. Dore Ashton, *Picasso on Art: A Selection of Views* (New York: Viking Press, 1972), 8.

6. Stone, *Dear Theo*, 383.

7. Annie Besant and C. W. Leadbeater, *Thought-Forms* (Wheaton, IL: Theosophical Publishing House, 1969), 23–24.

8. Isamu Noguchi, "On Gardens as Sculpture," A Sculptor's World, 1968 **www.noguchi.org/intextall.html** (18 March 1998).

9. Isamu Noguchi, *The Isamu Noguchi Garden Museum* (New York: Abrams, 1987), 37.

10. Henri Cartier-Bresson, *The World of Henri Cartier-Bresson* (New York: Viking Press, 1968), 3.

11. David Antin, "Video: The Distinctive Features of the Medium," in *Video Art* (Philadelphia: Institute for Contemporary Art, 1975), 64.

12. Quoted in David Sylvester, "Franz Kline 1910_1962: An Interview with David Sylvester," *Living Arts* 1 (Spring 1962): 4.

13. *Mltton Resnick*, directed by Sandy Brooke, in the video series *A World of Art: Works in Progress*, produce by Annenberg/CPB in conjunction with Oregon State University (Annenberg Media, 1997).

14. Quoted in Jonathan Fineberg, *Christo and Jeanne-Claude: On the Way to The Gates, Central Park, New York City* (New Haven: Yale University Press, in association with The Metropolitan Museum of Art, New York, 2004), 131.

CHAPTER 3

1. "Unframed Space," in "The Talk of the Town," *New Yorker* 26 (August 5, 1950): 16.

2. Jackson Pollock, Statement, *Possibilities* 1 (1947): unpaginated.

3. Andrea Lunsford, survey of 2,500 students, reported in "When Student Writers Use the Web: Problems and Issues," a public presentation, Oregon State University, 20 Feb. 1998.

4. Cited in Debra Aho Williamson, "College Students Embrace the Web," 10 Feb. 2006, iMedia Connection **www.imediaconnection.com/content/8237.asp** (26 Jan. 2008).

5. James Hall, *Dictionary of Subjects and Symbols in Art* (New York: Harper & Row, Icon Editions, 1974), 81, 85.

6. Henry Adams, *The Education of Henry Adams*, ed. Ernest Samuels (Boston: Riverside Editions, 1973), 380, 382.

7. Robert Wohl, "The Generation of 1914 and Modernism," in *Modernism: Challenges and Perspectives*, ed. Monique Chefdor, Ricardo Quinones, and Albert Wachtel (Urbana: University of Illinois Press, 1986), 72.

8. These positions, and others as well, can be discovered in Francis Frascina, *Pollock and After: The Critical Debate* (New York: Harper & Row, 1985).

9. Arianna Stassinopoulos Huffington, *Picasso: Creator and Destroyer* (New York: Simon & Schuster, 1988), 10.

CHAPTER 4

1. The student is quoting here from Andy Warhol and Pat Hackett, *Popism: The Warhol '60s* (New York: Harcourt Brace Jovanovich, 1980), 15.

2. Allan Kaprow, "The Legacy of Jackson Pollock," in *The Blurring of Art and Life*, ed. Jeff Kelley (Berkeley: University of California Press, 1993), 7.

3. Stephen Bennett Phillips, "Toward the Light," in *Sean Scully: Wall of Light* (New York: Rizzoli, in association with The Phillips Collection, 2005), 62.

4. Ibid.

5. Vincent van Gogh, Letter 571, 17 Jan. 1889, David Brooks, The Vincent van Gogh Gallery **www.vggallery.com/letters/to_theo_arles.htm** © R. G. Harrison (2 Feb. 2008).

6. Micheal Auping, "No Longer a Wall," in *Sean Scully: Wall of Light,* 24, 32.

7. "Hirshhorn Acquires Monumental Work by Roy Lichtenstein," press release, Hirshhorn Museum and Sculpture Garden, Washington, DC, September 2, 2003, **www.hirshhorn.si.edu/museum/press_release.asp?ID=45** (28 Nov. 2004).

8. Quoted in *Andy Warhol* exhibition catalogue (Stockholm: Moderna Museet, 1968), unpaginated.

9. Quoted in Ellen G. Landau, *Jackson Pollock* (New York: Abrams, 1989), 182.

INDEX

Boldface numbers indicate an illustration.

#328 (painting)(Reed), 4–5

A
Abstract art, 30, 66, 102–04, 113–14
Abstract expressionism, 65–68, 81,
   103–05, 107, 114
Acrylic painting, 57
Adams, Henry, 79–80
Adeline Art Dictionary, 78
After the End of Art (Danto), 97
Agee, James, 61
Agreement: pronoun, 132; subject-
   verb, 131–32
Albers, Josef, *Interaction of Color*, 42
Alligator Pears in a Basket
   (O'Keeffe), 38–40, **39**, 84
American art, 19–20, 81
*American Painting: From the Armory
   Show to the Depression* (Brown),
   19
Animism, 83

Antecedents, indefinite, 132–33
Antin, David, on video, 48
Apostrophes, 123
Architectural Index, 77
Architectural Week, 26
Architecture Links (website), 25
Art Abstracts, 76–77
Art after the End of Art (Danto), 4–5
Art Bulletin, footnote style, 88, 91–93
Art Full Text, 76
Art in America, footnotes in, 88
Art Index, 76
Art of Measurement (Dürer), **83**, 83–84
ARTbibliographies Modern, 77
Artchive (Harden), 25, 26
Artcyclopedia, 25, 26
Artforum, 13
Artists' statements, 70–71
Arts & Humanities Citation Index,
   77–78
Asymmetrical balance, 54, 63

Avery Index to Architectural Periodicals, 77

A.W. Mellon Lectures in the Fine Arts, 2

B

Balance, 28, 53–54, 61

Baroque art, 20, 28

Bartlett's Dictionary of Quotations, 66

Bedroom painting, 4–5

Besant, Annie, *Thought-Forms*, 44

BHA (Bibliography of the History of Art), 76, 77

Blogs, 106; citing as a source, 93–94

"Boat Gallery," 13

Bohr, Niels, 80

Bookmarking, 74

Brainstorming, in writing process, 100–01

Braque, Georges, 18

Brillo Boxes (Warhol), **1**, 1–2

Brookner, Anita, 118

Brown, Milton W., *American Painting: From the Armory Show to the Depression*, 19

Brushstroke (Lichtenstein), sculpture, 55, 102–104, **103**, 107, 113–14

Brutus and the Lictors (David), 120

Bryson, Norman, 121

Bucks County Barn (Sheeler), **18**, 18–20

Buglaj, Mikolai, *Racial Optical Illusion*, 55–56, **56**

Bunshaft, Gordon, 105, 107

Burial at Ornans (Courbet), 21–22, **22**, 23, 34, 55

C

Calder, Alexander, *Two Discs*, 105, **105**

Cartier-Bresson, Henri: *Gare St. Lazare*, 47, **48**; "the decisive moment," 47

Cast shadow, 39–40

Catalogs, 70–71

Ceramics, 57

Cézanne, Paul, 14; *Mont Sainte-Victoire* paintings, 15, 24, 33, **52**, 52–55, **53**, 79; *Still Life with Apples and a Pot of Primroses*, 25

Chador, 57

Chat rooms, 106

Chiaroscuro, 38–39

Chicago Manual of Style, 88–91

Christian West, 30

Christo and Jeanne-Claude: *The Gates*, 58, **59**; *Running Fence*, 50; *Surrounded Islands*, 50; *Umbrellas, Japan-U.S.A.*, 50–51; *Wrapped Reichstag*, 49–50, **50**, 58

Citation (*see also* footnotes), 87–94

Classical art, 28

Coffee Pot (Weems), 6–7, **7**, 100

Collage, 23, 58

College Art Association, review service, 78

Colons, 127

Color, 22, 23, 28, 32–33, 41–45, 56, 62; analogous hues, 42, 62; color wheel, 41–42; complementary hues, 41–42; cool colors, 42; local, 44; optical, 44; primary colors, 41; quality of reproduction, 23; secondary colors, 41; shade, 41; symbolic meaning of, 44; tint, 41; warm colors, 42

Colosseum, Rome, 73–75

Comma splices, 124–25

Commas, 123–24

Commercial time, 48

Comparative essays, 18–21, 110–13; continuity and change in, 21

Complexity in art, 16–17

Composition, 37

Computer media, 51

Conclusions, 72

Concrete language, 135

Consistency: diction, 134; verb tense, 134

Context, 11–13, 14–15, 27, 79–85

Cornell Farm (Hicks), **19**, 19–20

Correlative expressions (both/and, not only/but also), 133–34
Countess of Chinchón (Goya), 110–11, **111**
Courbet, Gustave, 80; *Burial at Ornans*, 21–22, **22**, 23, 34, 55; *Woman with a Parrot*, 24–25
Courbeton, Micault de, 117
Crivelli, Carlo, *Crucifixion*, 30–31, **32**, 33–35, 54, 57, 77, 79, 86
Crucifixion (Crivelli), 30–31, **32**, 33–35, 54, 57, 77, 79, 86
Crucifixion with Saints (Perugino), 30–32, **31**, 33–34, 41, 53–54, 57, 86
Cubism, 18–20, 23; historical context of, 79–80
Curriculum vitae, 70, 71

D
Danto, Arthur C., 1–2, 4–6, 26; *After the End of Art*, 97
Dashes, 128
David, Jacques Louis, 80; *Brutus and the Lictors*, 120; *Death of Socrates*, 120; *Madame Trudaine*, 110–11, **112**, 117–21; *Marat at His Last Breath*, 120; *Oath of the Horatii*, 120; *Tennis Court Oath*, 120
Death of Socrates (David), 120
Description, in writing process, 58–59
Design, principles of, 52–56
Diamond, William (Regional Administrator of the General Services Administration), 11
Dickens, Charles, 118
Diction, 134
Dictionary of Art and Artists (Murray), 79
Dictionary of Art Terms and Techniques (Mayer), 78
Dictionary of Art (Turner), 78
Dictionary of Subjects and Symbols in Art (Hall), 79
Digital photography, 51

Dimensions, 19–20, 36
Downtrodden (Kollwitz), **40**, 40–41, 84
Draftsman Drawing a Reclining Nude (Dürer), **83**, 83–84
Drawing, 57
Duchamp, Marcel, *Nude Descending a Staircase*, 66
Dürer, Albrecht: *Art of Measurement*, **83**, 83–84; *Draftsman Drawing a Reclining Nude*, **83**, 83–84

E
E-mail: citing as a source, 94; discussion groups, 106–08; pitfalls of, 108
Editing, 115–17
Einstein, Alfred, Special Theory of Relativity, 80
Ellipses, 130
Emotional response, 3
Evans, Walker, 59–61; *Washroom and Dining Area of Floyd Burroughs's Home*, **60**, 60–61

F
Feminist art criticism, 83–84
Fiber art, 57
Film techniques, 49
Fine Arts Museum of San Francisco, ImageBase, 25
Firefox, 73
First Love, 17
Footnotes, 88–94; *Art Bulletin* style, 88, 91–93; *Chicago Manual* style, 88–91; citing Internet sources, 93–94
Foreign phases, 126
Form, 33
Formal analysis and description, in writing process, 3, 113–15
Formal elements, 29, 33–51, 52, 62–63
French Academy, 15

French Revolution, 118
Full Fathom Five (Pollock), 30,
  64–68, **65**, 69, 71, 81, 98–100,
  113, 114

G
Gare Saint-Lazare (Monet), 35–37, **36**
Gare St. Lazare (Cartier-Bresson),
  47, **48**
Gates (Christo and Jeanne-Claude),
  58, **59**
Gaze, 83–84
Gehry, Frank, 13; Solomon R.
  Guggenheim Museum, Bilbao,
  12, 13
Gender, and pronoun use, 132
Giotto, 80
Glass, 57
Golden section, 54–55
Google, 25, 73, 74
Gouache, 57
Goya, Francisco, *Countess of
  Chinchón*, 40, 110–11, **111**
Great Buildings Collection (website),
  25–26
Green, Tyler, 94
Grove Dictionary of Art Online
  (Turner), 78
Guardians of the Secret (Pollock), 114
Guggenheim, Peggy, 69
Gursky, Andreas, *Untitled V*, 51, **51**

H
Hall, James, *Dictionary of Subjects
  and Symbols in Art*, 79
Harden, Mark, 25, 26
Harmsen, Leif (Art History Research
  Centre), 24
Hicks, Edward, *The Cornell Farm*,
  19, 19–20
High Renaissance, 20
Highlights, 39
Hirshhorn Museum and Sculpture
  Garden, 102–05, 113
Hitchcock, Alfred, 4; *Vertigo*, 26

Howe, Jeffrey, Architecture Links, 25
Huffington, Arianna Sassinopoulos,
  Picasso: Creator and Destroyer, 84
Humanism, 80

I
Iconography, 30
ImageBase, Fine Arts Museum of San
  Francisco, 25
Images: choosing, 9–27; meaning of,
  6–7
Impression Sunrise (Monet), 25
Impressionist painting, 14–15
Indexes, consulting, 76–78
Infinitives, split, 126
"Inside the White Cube" (O'Doherty),
  13, 64, 98
*Insurrection! (Our Tools Were Rudi-
  mentary, Yet We Pressed On)*
  (Walker), 85, **85**
Intention, 3, 6
Interaction of Color (Albers), 42
Internet, 23–26, 72–74; footnoting,
  93–94
Internet-based art, 50
Internet Explorer, 73
Interpretation, 3, 8
Isamu Noguchi Garden Museum,
  Long Island City, Queens, NY, **46**,
  46–47, 55, 74
Islam, 57

J
Jacob R. Javits Federal Building, 11
Japanese gardens, 46–47
Judy's Bedroom (Reed), 5

K
Kaprow, Allan, on Jackson Pollock,
  107
Kline, Franz, *Mahoning*, **37**, 37–38, 54
Kollwitz, Käthe, *The Downtrodden*,
  40, 40–41, 84
Kongo, 81–83
Krasner, Lee, 66

L

Landscape, 20, 33–35
Lautenschlager, Sharon, 117–21
Leadbeater, C.W., *Thought-Forms*, 44
Learning to Look (Taylor), 30–32,
    77, 86
Let Us Now Praise Famous Men
    (Evans and Agee), 61
Library research, 73–78
Lichtenstein, Roy: *Brushstroke*, 55,
    102–04, **103**, 107, 113–14; *Little
    Big Painting*, **104**
Light and dark, 38–41, 45, 110
Line, 28, 33–35
Listserves, 106
Little Big Painting (Lichtenstein), **104**
Louis XV, king of France, 84
Louvre (Paris), 117

M

Madame Chagrin, 117
Madame Trudaine (David), 110–11,
    112, 117–21
Mahoning (Kline), **37**, 37–38, 54
Mallen, Enrique, Picasso Project, 25
Malraux, André, "Museum without
    Walls," 22
Manet, Edouard, 14, 16
Mannerism, 20
Mapping, in writing process, 101
Marat at His Last Breath (David), 120
Marmottan Museum (Paris), 25
Masculinist gaze, 83–84
Masterpiece (Zola), 14, 16
Master's gaze, 84
Mayer, Ralph, *Dictionary of Art
    Terms and Techniques*, 78
McLaughlin, John, 4
Meaning, 30–31, 59
Media, 29, 57–58, 59, 63; computer,
    51; linear, 49; spatial, 49; temporal,
    49
Media choice in art, 6
Media Farm, 74
Metal art, 57

Metasearch engines, 73–74
Metropolitan Museum of Art, 15, 24
Michelangelo, 20; Sistine Chapel, 58
Minkisi minkonde, 84
Minkonde, 82
Modern art, 19, 104–05
Modern Art Notes (Green), 94
Modifiers, dangling, 131
Monet, Claude, 14, 15; *Gare Saint-
    Lazare, Paris*, 35–37, **36**;
    Impression Sunrise, 25
Mont Sainte-Victoire paintings
    (Cézanne), 15, 24, 33, 34, **52**,
    52–55, **53**, 79
Murray, Linda, *Dictionary of Art and
    Artists*, 79
Musée d'Orsay (Paris), 15, 21
Museum of Fine Arts (Houston), 74
Museum of Modern Art (New York
    City), 64, 68, 69
Museums: arrangement and grouping
    of works in, 15–16; educational
    mission of, 15–16; people's per-
    ceptions of, 9–11; without walls,
    22–26
"Museums without Walls" (Malraux),
    22; and the Internet, 23–26

N

National Gallery, Washington, D.C.,
    24
Neoclassicism, 20, 80
Neshat, Shirin, *Rapture*, 57, **58**
Netscape Navigator, 73
Newsgroups, 106
NGAKids, 24
Night Café (van Gogh), 42–44, **43**, 45,
    75, 98
NikeTown, 51
Nkisi nkonde, 81–82, **82**
Noguchi, Isamu, Isamu Noguchi Gar-
    den Museum, **46**, 46–47, 55, 74
Novak, Kim, 4
Nude Descending a Staircase
    (Duchamp), 66

O

Oath of the Horatii (David), 120
O'Doherty, Brian, "Inside the White
Cube," 13, 98
Oil painting, 57
O'Keeffe, Georgia, *Alligator Pears in
a Basket*, 38–40, **39**, 84
Oklahoma City bombing, 13
On-line research, 72–74
"One-person" show, 15
Outlines, 98–99
Oxford English Dictionary, 66

P

Painting media, 57
Parentheses, 129
Parthenon, 45
Perspective, 35–37, 62; laws of, 16;
vanishing point in, 35
Perugino, Pietro, *Crucifixion with
Saints*, 30–32, **31**, 33–34, 41,
53–54, 57, 86
Phidias and workshop, *Three
Goddesses*, **45**, 45–46
Phillips, Stephen Bennett, 110
Photodocumentation, 49–50
Photography, 47, 57–58, 59–61;
digital, 51
Picasso: Creator and Destroyer
(Picasso), 84
Picasso, Pablo, 16, 18, 20; *Woman
with Book*, 42–44, 56, 84, 98,
back cover
Picasso Project (website), 25
Plagiarism, 87
Pollock, Jackson, 30, 76, 105, 107;
Full Fathom Five, 30, 64–68, **65**,
69, 71, 81, 98, 99, 100, 113, 114;
Guardians of the Secret, 114;
statement in *Possibilities*, 70;
Untitled, 30
Pop art, 1–2, 103–04, 107, 114
Possibilities, Pollock's statement
in, 70
Postmodern art, 28

Prewriting, in writing process,
101–06
Princeton University, 2
Principles of design, 29, 52–56, 62
Printmaking, 40, 57
Pronouns, 132
Proportion, 41, 54–55
Psychic automatism (Surrealism), 69

Q

Questioning art, 3, 8
Quoting, 86–87, 129–30

R

*RAA (Répertoire d'art et d'Archeolo-
gie)*, 76
Race relations, 84
Racial Optical Illusion (Buglaj),
55–56, **56**
Radial balance, 54
Rapture (Neshat), 57, **58**
Realism, 80
Reductive attempts in writing about
images, 7–8
Reed, David, 4–6, 26; "Scottie's
Place / Judy's Place," 26
Relative value, 39
Rembrandt van Rijn, 40
Renaissance, 80
Renaissance Italy, 38
Repetition, 52–53, 63
Representation, 30
Reproductions, 22–23; on the Web,
24–25
Research papers, 71–72
Resnick, Milton, 54
Revision, 115–17
Rhythm, 28, 52–53
Rifkin, Ned, Director, Hirshhorn
Museum and Sculpture Garden,
113–14
*RILA (Répertoire international de
la littérature de l'art)*, 76
Romantic art, 28
Romanticism, 20

Room for St. John of the Cross
(Viola), 48–49, **49**, 55
Running Fence (Christo and Jeanne-
Claude), 50

S
Safari, 73
Salon des Refusés, 15
San Francisco, Fine Arts Museum
of, 24
Sayre, Henry, 2, 6
Scale, 55–56, 63
Schnapper, Antoine, 120
"Scottie's Place / Judy's Place"
(Reed), 26
Scully, Sean, 108–09, **front cover**;
Wall of Light exhibition, 110
Sculpture, 28, 30, 45–46, 57
Search engines, 25, 73–74
Semi-colons, 127–28
Sentences: fragments, 127; run-on,
125
Serra, Richard: *Snake*, **12**, 13; *Tilted
Arc*, **10**, **11**, 11–13, 21, 49
Shaker art, 19
Shakespeare, William, *Tempest*, 67, 68
Shape, 35–38, 54, 63
Sheeler, Charles, *Bucks County Barn*,
18, 18–20
Silhouette, Etienne de, 84
Silhouette as art form, 84–85
Sisley, Alfred, 14
Snake (Serra), **12**, 13
Social history, 81–83
Solomon R. Guggenheim Museum,
Bilbao (Gehry), **12**, 13
Solomon R. Guggenheim Museum,
New York (Wright), 105
Space, 35–38
Spelling, common mistakes, 115,
135–36
*Still Life with Apples and a Pot of
Primroses* (Cézanne), 25
Subject matter, 29–33, 59, 62
Surrealists, 69

Surrounded Islands (Christo and
Jeanne-Claude), 50

T
Tale of Two Cities (Dickens), 118
Tate Museum (London), 110
Taylor, Joshua C., *Learning to Look*,
30–32, 77, 86
Television, 48
Tempera, 57
Tempest (Shakespeare), 67, 68
Tennis Court Oath (David), 120
Texture, 45, 62
That and *Which*, distinguishing
between, 125
Thesis statements, 20, 113–15
Thought-Forms (Besant and
Leadbeater), 44
Three-dimensional space, 3, 35–37
Three Goddesses (Phidias), **45**,
45–46
Tilted Arc (Serra), **10**, **11**, 11–13, 21, 49
Time, 45–51, 62
Titles, 64–68, 125–26
Trudaine, Charles Louis, 120
Trudaine, Charles Michel, 120
Trudaine, Madame Charles
Louis, 117
Turner, Jane, editor: *Dictionary of Art*,
78; *Grove Dictionary of Art
Online*, 78
*Twenty Thousand Leagues Under the
Sea* (Verne), 66
Two Bedrooms in San Francisco
(Reed), 5
Two-dimensional space, 35–37, 38
Two Discs (Calder), 105, **105**

U
Umbrellas, Japan-U.S.A. (Christo and
Jeanne-Claude), 50–51
Uncertainty, toleration of, 4
Unity, 56
Untitled (Pollock), 30
Untitled V (Gursky), **51**, 51

V

van Gogh, Theo, 42, 44, 110
van Gogh, Vincent, 109; *Night Café*, 42–44, **43**, 45, 75, 98; *Vincent's Chair with Pipe*, 109–10, **back cover**
Vanishing point, 35
Variety, 56, 65
Venus of Willendorf, 66
Verb tense consistency, 134
Verne, Jules, *Twenty Thousand Leagues Under the Sea*, 66
Vertigo (film) (Hitchcock), 4, 26
Video art, 28, 47–49, 57–58
Vincent (Scully), 108–09, **front cover**
Vincent's Chair with Pipe (van Gogh), 109–10, **back cover**
Viola, Bill, *Room for St. John of the Cross*, 48–49, **49**, 55
Visual elements of art, 6

W

Walker, Kara, 84; *Insurrection! (Our Tools Were Rudimentary, Yet We Pressed On)*, 85, **85**
Wall of Light exhibition (Scully), 110
Walter, Marie-Thérèse, 43–44, 56, 84
Warhol, Andy, 1–2, 103–04, 114
Washroom and Dining Area of Floyd Burroughs's Home (Evans), **60**, 60–61
Watercolor, 57
Watson, Richard, 59–61
Web browsers, 73
Web Gallery of Art, 25
Weems, Carrie Mae, *Coffee Pot*, 6–7, **7**, 100

Which and *That*, distinguishing between, 125
Wikipedia, 73
Wilder, Nicholas, 4
Wohl, Robert, 80
Woman with a Parrot (Courbet), 24–25
Woman with Book (Picasso), 42–44, 56, 84, 98, **back cover**
Words and their relation to images, 6
Work of art, defining, 1–2
World of Art, (Sayre), 2, 6
World War I, 79
World Wide Web, 23–26, 72–74, 77, 106; citing as a source, 93–94
Wrapped Reichstag (Christo and Jeanne-Claude), 49–50, **50**, 58
Wright, Frank Lloyd, Solomon R. Guggenheim Museum, New York, 105
Writing process, 4, 95–121; brainstorming in, 100–01; description, 58–59; developing thesis in, 113–15; as a dialogue, 16–17; as exploration, 17; focusing your discussion, 98–100; formal description in, 98–100; mapping in, 101; note taking, 95–98; on-line, 106–08; prewriting in, 101–06; revising and editing in, 115–17; vocabulary, 28–29

Y

Yahoo!, 25, 73

Z

Zola, Emile, *The Masterpiece*, 14, 16